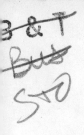

Patrick Moore's
Color Star Atlas

Patrick Moore's
Color Star Atlas

Crown Publishers Inc.
New York

CONTENTS

Crown Publishers, Inc.,
419 Park Avenue South,
New York, N.Y. 10016

Produced in association with
Mitchell Beazley Publishers Limited
Artists' House
14–15 Manette Street
London, W1V 5LB

First published in the United States in 1973

© Mitchell Beazley Publishers Limited 1973

Star Maps (pp 34–5, 38–9, 42–3, 46–7, 50–1, 54–5, 58–9, 62–3) © Hallwag Berne 1973

Library of Congress Catalog Card Number 73-88403

ISBN 0 517 514036
Printed in the Netherlands.

Frontispiece Eta Carinæ and its associated nebulosity. Hot stars are surrounded by gas and dust which is illuminated by their activity. Photographed at the Cape Observatory.

Illustration credits

Mount Wilson and Palomar Observatories Andromeda Spiral, 9; DQ Herculis, 20; NGC 4725, 21; Nebulæ, 22, 23; Globular cluster, 24; NGC 205, NGC 7219, NGC 3504, M.81, M.33, Galaxy in Hercules, 30; Spiral galaxy M.94, Gaseous nebula IC 443, 36; Loose spiral galaxy, Open spiral, 40; Rosette nebula, 41; Crab nebula, 44; Pleiades, 45; All photos, 48–9; Orion nebula, 52; Planetary nebula, Horse's head nebula, 53; All photos, 56; Star clouds, 57; All photos, 60–1; All photos, 64; Barred spiral, 65. *U.S. Naval Observatory* Globular cluster, 36; Whirlpool galaxy, 37; Irregular galaxy, 40; Nucleus of Andromeda spiral, 44; Star fields in Milky Way, 52; M.104 in Virgo, 57. *Patrick Moore Collection* Cassiopeia, 17; Observatories, 68–9. *Cape Observatory* Eta Carinæ, frontispiece, 65. *Lick Observatory* M.87, NGC 7479, 31. *Radcliffe Observatory* 30 Doradus, 65. *Alan Williams* Gemini, 17. *T.J.C.A. Moseley* HR Delphini, 20.

Diagrams by Colin Rose
Charts by Colin Rose and Andrew Farmer
Cover photograph by Selsey Photographic

FOREWORD

We are living in the Space Age. Not so very long ago, astronomy was regarded as a purely academic subject; nowadays it has become part of our everyday life. Artificial satellites are circling the Earth, and probe vehicles have been sent out to the planets; men have reached the Moon, and already there are plans to set up scientific bases there. The situation today is entirely different from anything which could have been pictured a few decades ago.

Perhaps because of all this activity, popular attention is focused mainly upon the bodies of the Solar System—that is to say, the Sun, the Moon and the planets. Yet the Solar System is only a very small part of the universe as a whole, and it would be wrong to over-estimate its importance in the general scheme of things. Our Galaxy contains at least 100,000 million suns, many of which may well have planetary systems of their own. It would be both conceited and illogical to believe that we are the only intelligent beings in the cosmos.

The aim of this atlas is to give a general introduction to the stellar universe. The stars are suns; each has its own characteristics, and each has its own points of special interest. The variety of objects in the Galaxy is starting to seem almost endless, and there have been startling developments during the past few years. The story of astronomical discovery is not over. Indeed, it may be only just beginning.

Patrick Moore

INTRODUCTION TO THE STARS

Look up into the sky on any dark, cloudless night, and you will see many hundreds of stars. Some are much brighter than others, but all seem to be tiny, twinkling points, and it is not hard to see why our ancestors believed them to be lamps attached to an invisible crystal sphere revolving round the Earth once a day. Not until astronomy became a true science was it realized that the stars are suns, some of which are far larger, hotter and more powerful than our own Sun.

There is only one reason why the stars appear so small: they are immensely remote. If the Earth–Sun distance is represented by one inch, even the nearest star will be more than four miles away, and most of the rest are much more distant still. Indeed, the mile is too short a unit to be useful in discussing stellar distances, and astronomers prefer to use the light-year, which is equal to the distance travelled by a ray of light in one year. Since light moves at 186,000 miles per second, a light-year is equivalent to almost six million million miles. The nearest star is more than four light-years away, and we see it as it used to be more than four years ago. Once we look beyond the Solar System—our own particular region of the universe—our view is bound to be very much out of date.

The Sun is a huge globe of hot gas, shining because it is producing energy. The same is true of the stars, but not of the planets—Mercury, Venus, Mars, Jupiter, Saturn, Uranus, Neptune and Pluto—which move round the Sun in the same way as the Earth, and shine entirely by reflecting the Sun's light. Moreover, the planets seem to move around against the starry background, and shift from constellation to constellation. This is because they are relatively close at hand, whereas the stars are so remote that their individual or 'proper' motions are very slight. To all intents and purposes, the constellation patterns we see today are the same as those which must have been seen in the days of King Alfred, Julius Cæsar or the ancient Egyptian builders of the pyramids.

When seen through even a moderate telescope, a planet will reveal considerable detail. Mars has its polar caps and its dark regions; Jupiter has its belts and spots, while Saturn is surrounded by a superb system of rings. Yet no telescope yet built will show a star as anything but a point of light, and most of our present-day knowledge has been gained by using instruments built upon the principle of the spectroscope. The light from the stars is split up, and we can find out what substances exist there.

A star may seem brilliant either because it is relatively close on the scale of the universe, or because it is really very powerful. Apparent brightness is measured upon what is called the 'magnitude' scale, which works rather in the manner of a golfer's handicap; the more brilliant performers have the lower magnitudes. A really bright star is classed as being of the 1st magnitude; 2nd-magnitude stars are fainter, and so on. The dimmest stars normally visible with the naked eye are of the 6th magnitude, but optical aid increases the range, and the world's largest telescopes can photograph stars down to magnitude +23.

Yet apparent magnitude is not necessarily a reliable guide to the star's luminosity, as one obvious example will show. Sirius, which shines as the brightest star in the entire sky (magnitude −1.43; that is to say, well above zero magnitude), is 26 times as powerful as the Sun, and is 8.6 light-years away from us. Rigel, in Orion, is not so conspicuous; its magnitude is only 0.2—but it has 50,000 times the Sun's luminosity, and is so remote that its light takes about 900 years to reach us. Were Rigel as close as Sirius, it would cast shadows. The most powerful star known to us, S Doradûs, is a million times more luminous than the Sun, but it is so far away that it cannot be seen with the naked eye. On the other hand, we also know of stars which are comparatively feeble. If we represent the Sun by a pocket torch, the other stars will range from searchlights down to glow-worms.

The sizes of the stars show just as great a range

Some of the huge giants have diameters amounting to hundreds of millions of miles; for instance Betelgeux, a red star in the constellation of Orion, is big enough to hold the entire orbit of the Earth round the Sun. At the other end of the scale, there are stars which are smaller than the Earth. This is not to say that they are planets; there is an essential difference between a planet and a star.

Any casual glance will show that the stars are not all of the same colour. Some are bluish or white, others yellow, and others orange or red. These differences are due to real differences in surface temperature. The temperature of the Sun's surface is 6,000 degrees Centigrade; blue and white stars are hotter, while orange and red stars are cooler. Once again our yellow, undistinguished Sun comes about half way down the scale.

Everyone must have heard the old rhyme which begins 'Twinkle, twinkle, little star . . .' It is true that the stars do seem to twinkle, but the effect is due entirely to the unsteady atmosphere of the Earth, and has nothing directly to do with the stars themselves. This is easily shown by comparing two bright stars, one which is near the horizon and the other which is near the zenith, or overhead point. The lower star will twinkle much more obviously, because its light is coming to us through a thicker layer of atmosphere. Sirius twinkles particularly violently, because it is so brilliant. Planets, which show up as small disks rather than as mere points, twinkle appreciably less than stars.

There are stars of many kinds. Most of them— including the Sun, fortunately for us—shine steadily, but some are variable in light. We also have double or binary stars, and even multiple groups; there are clusters of stars, such as the famous Pleiades or Seven Sisters, and in addition the Galaxy contains huge clouds of rarefied gas and dust which we call nebulæ. Now and then we witness tremendous outbursts, when a formerly faint star will flare up to many times its normal brilliancy, remaining bright for a few days or weeks before sinking back to its old state. Many of these so-called novæ or 'temporary stars' have been discovered by amateur astronomers. Much more infrequently we can see a star suffer a catastrophic explosion, ending up as a small, super-dense stellar remnant together with a patch of expanding gas. This is known as a supernova outburst; the last to be seen in our Galaxy appeared as long ago as 1604, but they are so powerful that they can be observed in other systems millions of light-years away.

The system in which we live, our own particular Galaxy, is extremely large. It has an overall diameter of 100,000 light-years, but its maximum width is less than one-third of this value; the Galaxy is flattened, and has been compared with the shape of two fried eggs clapped together back to back! If it could be seen 'from above' or 'below' it would appear as a rather loose spiral, resembling a catherine-wheel. It is in rotation; our Sun, like the other stars, is moving round the galactic centre, taking the Earth and all the other planets with it.

Virtually all the naked-eye objects in the sky belong to our Galaxy. The only exceptions are the two Clouds of Magellan in the southern hemisphere and the Andromeda Spiral in the north, which are independent galaxies. With telescopes, many other galaxies can be seen, and it has been estimated that our most powerful instruments are capable of photographing about 1,000 million of them, though most appear as nothing more than tiny patches of light. Just as the Earth is an ordinary planet, and the Sun an ordinary star, so our system is an ordinary galaxy; it may be rather above the average in size and mass, but it is not exceptional.

Certainly we have come a long way from the time when the Earth was regarded as the centre of the universe. This leads on to another fascinating problem: if the stars are suns, then can they too be attended by systems of planets? And if so, can any of these planets be inhabited?

When we start to search for life on other worlds, it is natural to begin with the planets in our Solar System. Unfortunately the prospects do not appear to be good. For life to exist, there must be a reasonably equable temperature, the right kind of atmosphere, and a supply of water. These conditions are not found on any of our neighbour worlds. The only member of the Sun's family, apart from the Earth, which might conceivably support life is Mars; and even on Mars we cannot expect to find anything more advanced than very lowly organic matter. Evidence from the recent space-probes seems to indicate that even this is unlikely. Of course, there have been many suggestions that there may be life of entirely alien form, capable of existing under alien conditions; but we have to admit that the evidence is against anything of the sort.

However, let us repeat that the Sun is an ordinary star, essentially similar to many of its 100,000 million companions in the Galaxy. There seems no reason to doubt that other planetary families are common. The trouble is that we cannot see them directly; a planet is much smaller than a normal star, and has no light of its own, so that even a large planet moving round a nearby star would be hopelessly beyond the range of our telescopes. The evidence which we have is necessarily indirect; but it would be both conceited and unscientific to believe that there is no other intelligent life. Whether we will ever be able to obtain positive proof remains to be seen.

Origins of the Universe

Of all the questions facing modern science, perhaps the most fascinating—and certainly the most fundamental—is that of the origin of the universe. Many theories have been put forward, and the arguments which have raged during the past few decades have often become heated, but we cannot yet claim that we have any real idea of the truth.

We have to deal with a universe which contains galaxies, stars, planets and moons. The scale is immense in both dimension and time. We know of galaxies which are thousands of millions of light-years from us, and according to the best available evidence the entire universe is in a state of expansion; each group of galaxies is receding from each other group. We cannot tell whether the universe is finite or infinite, but at least we have some clues as to its age.

We can show that the age of the Earth is between 4,000 and 5,000 million years. This estimate may be regarded as reliable, since several lines of investigation lead to the same result. Samples obtained from the lunar crust, brought back by recent expeditions to the Moon, indicate that the Moon and the Earth are about equally old, and the same is presumably true of the other planets. It follows that the Sun is certainly at least 5,000 million years old, perhaps rather more.

Unquestionably there are some stars which are at least twice as old as the Sun, and we cannot put the age of the universe at less than 10,000 million years. This is the minimum figure, but it seems to be a definite underestimate. What we have to decide is whether the universe began at one particular moment in time, more than 10,000 million years ago, or whether it has always existed and, having no limits in the past, will have a limitless future.

According to the 'big bang', or evolutionary, theory, the matter in the universe was created suddenly in one particular area. This so-called 'primæval atom' exploded, and sent material hurtling outward in all directions. The initially very high temperature fell steadily, and after a while galaxies began to form out of the chaos; stars then condensed out of the material in these galaxies, and the planets of our Solar System were produced by accretion from a cloud of matter which was associated with the Sun. Thus the universe had a definite moment of birth, and will eventually die.

This idea was challenged in the late 1940s by a group of scientists at Cambridge, headed by H. Bondi and T. Gold. Their 'steady-state' theory dispensed with a sudden creation; they assumed that the universe has always existed, and will exist forever. As old stars and galaxies die, new material is produced spontaneously out of nothing, and in the course of time fresh galaxies are formed. The continuous creation of matter takes place much too slowly to be checked by observational methods, which makes the theory very difficult to prove or disprove.

It has been found that the rate of recession of a galaxy depends upon its distance from us; the farther away it is, the faster it goes. If the evidence is to be believed, there are some very remote objects known as quasars (possibly, though not certainly, special kinds of galaxies), which are moving away at more than 90 per cent of the velocity of light. If this law holds good for still greater distances, there must come a distance at which a galaxy is receding at the full speed of light, in which case we could never see it—and this would give a boundary to the observable universe. The steady-state theory claimed that new galaxies, produced from the spontaneously-created matter, would take the place of the galaxies which passed beyond the boundary of the observable universe, so that the overall view would always be much the same as it is at the present time.

However, this would mean that certain laws of distribution of very remote objects would have to be followed, and this has not been confirmed by modern techniques. The steady-state theory in its original form has now been abandoned by almost all authorities. Yet this does not necessarily mean that the 'big bang' idea is correct. It may well be that the present expansion of the universe will not continue indefinitely, and will be followed by a period of contraction, ending when all the galaxies come together once more; this in turn will be succeeded by a new expansion. The universe will be in a state of oscillation, and will be 're-born' approximately every 60,000 million years.

At the moment we cannot decide between these rival theories, and we must admit that all of them may be very wide of the mark. Moreover, nobody has ever been able to explain just *how* the material in the universe came into being. We are discussing the development of the universe rather than its origin, and we are no nearer toward solving the fundamental problem of the creation of the universe than were our ancestors who believed that the Earth lay in the centre of the cosmos.

The Andromeda Spiral *right* One of the nearest of our neighbour galaxies. It is a system larger than our own, and contains more than our Galaxy's quota of 100,000 million stars. It is 2.2 million light-years away.

Mapping the Stars

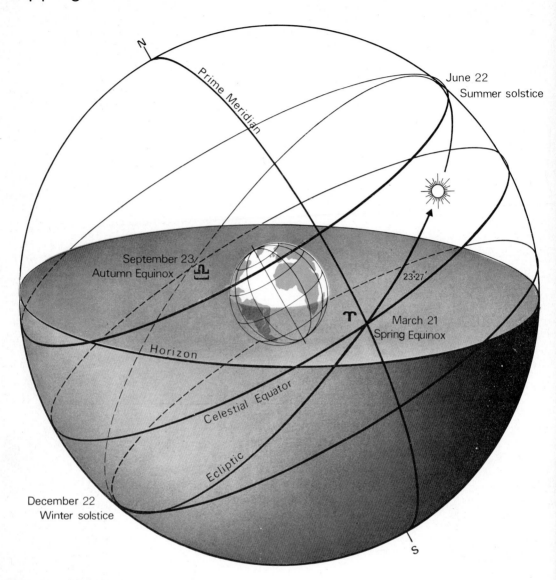

The Celestial Sphere *above* Ancient astronomers believed the sky to be solid. The idea of a 'celestial sphere', as shown in the diagram, is very convenient. The celestial equator is the projection of the Earth's equator on to the celestial sphere; the poles are indicated by the direction of the axis of rotation. The plane of the Earth's orbit is the ecliptic—also defined as the apparent yearly path of the Sun among the stars.

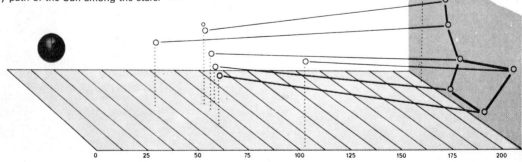

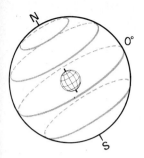

Poles and Equator *left*
The diagram shows the celestial poles, indicated by the direction of the Earth's axis, and also the equator; just as the terrestrial equator divides the Earth into two hemispheres, so the celestial equator divides the sky into halves.

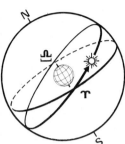

The Ecliptic and the Equinoxes *left* The ecliptic is the projection of the plane of the Earth's orbit on to the celestial sphere; the equinoxes are the points of intersection between the ecliptic and the celestial equator.

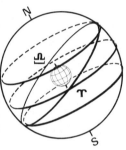

The Solstices *left* About 22 June and 22 December respectively, the Sun reaches its northernmost and southernmost points in the sky. The Sun is then 23°27' from the celestial equator, since the Earth's equator is inclined by this amount to the orbital plane.

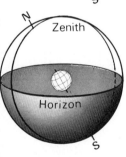

Horizon and Meridian *left* The observer's horizon and meridian are shown. The meridian is the great circle on the celestial sphere which passes through both poles and also through the overhead point, known as the observer's zenith.

Star Distances *left* We now know that the stars are by no means at the same distance from us, and that the stars in any particular constellation are not necessarily associated with each other. The diagram shows the seven stars of the Great Bear or Plough, drawn at their correct relative distances from us. Two of the stars (Alkaid and Dubhe) are much more remote than the rest, and simply lie in the same direction as seen from the Earth.

Measuring Distances by Parallax *right* The Sun is represented by S: the Earth is shown at A and B, on opposite sides of its orbit. Because the Earth–Sun distance is 93 million miles, AB = 186 million miles. The star X, relatively close to us, will appear in a different position according to whether it is observed from A or B. Its apparent shift over six months enables its actual distance to be calculated.

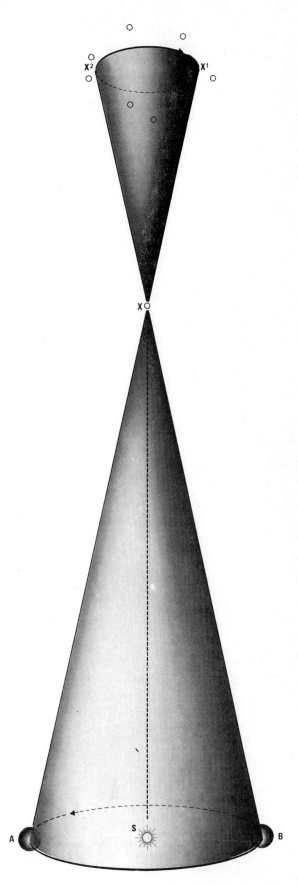

Motions of the Stars

The apparent rotation of the sky is due to the real rotation of the Earth on its axis. The Sun, Moon and planets share in this diurnal rotation, though because of their closeness they also have individual movements of their own.

The positions of the stars on the celestial sphere are measured by *declination* and *right ascension*. Declination is the star's angular distance from the celestial equator, as reckoned from the centre of the Earth; it is equivalent to latitude on the Earth's surface. The north celestial pole has declination +90°.

Right ascension is reckoned from the spring equinox or First Point of Aries—that is to say, the position in the sky at which the Sun crosses the equator in its movement from south to north (around 22 March each year). The First Point of Aries—which is not marked by any bright star—culminates, or reaches its greatest altitude above the horizon, once a day. The right ascension of a star is given by the time interval between the culmination of the First Point of Aries and the culmination of the star. Thus Rigel culminates 5 hours, 12 minutes after the First Point has done so—the right ascension of Rigel is 5 h 12 m.

An observer at the Earth's north pole has a permanent view of the northern hemisphere of the sky, and any star with a southerly declination never rises. The converse is true for an observer at the south pole, while for an observer on the Earth's equator, both poles of the sky lie on the horizon. Only from the equator can the entire sky be seen. From Europe, the Southern Cross never rises; in New Zealand the Great Bear is out of view.

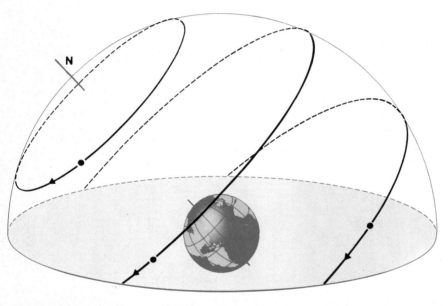

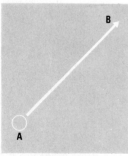

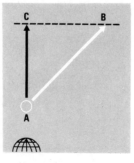

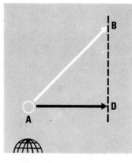

The Diurnal Motions of the Stars *left* All the stars appear to describe circles round the celestial pole, completing one circuit in 23 h 56 m 4 s— that is to say, the length of the Earth's rotation. Only the celestial poles show no diurnal motion. The altitude of the pole is the same as the latitude of the observer; thus from Selsey in Sussex (latitude 50° 44′) the altitude of the north celestial pole is 50° 44′. This can be estimated from the altitude of Polaris, the Pole Star, whose declination exceeds +89°. There is no bright star near the south celestial pole.

Radial and Transverse Velocity *left* The motion of the stars across the line of sight, known as proper motion, causes an apparent, measurable shift against the background of more remote stars; even so, the star with the greatest known proper motion (Barnard's Star, at six light-years) takes 180 years to cover a distance equal to the apparent diameter of the full moon. The towards-or-away motion (radial motion) is measured spectro-scopically, and does not produce an actual, measurable shift.

True Motion *above* The line AB shows the true motion of the star in space over a period of time. This is the combination of transverse and radial motion.

Radial Motion *above* Indicated by AC, measured by spectroscopy. Its value is negative if the star is approaching, positive if receding.

Transverse Motion *above* Shown by AD; this produces an apparent shift (the proper motion) of a star against the background of stars which are more remote.

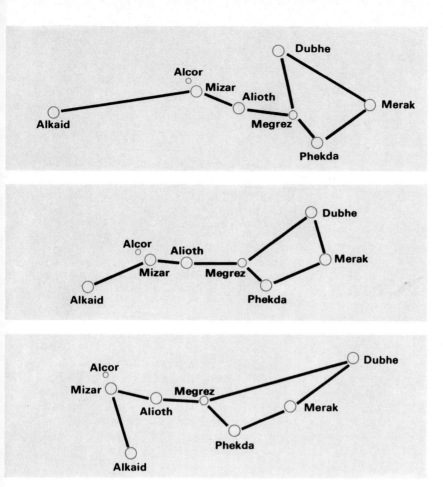

Proper Motion *left* The proper motions of the stars are so slight that they are not noticeable with the naked eye even over periods of centuries, but over a sufficient length of time they mount up. The diagrams here show the seven stars of the Great Bear as they would have appeared 100,000 years ago (top), as they appear today (middle) and as they will be in 100,000 years' time (bottom). The distances of these stars range from 68 light-years for Alioth to 210 light-years for Alkaid. Five of the stars are moving in much the same direction, but the two most distant members of the group, Alkaid and Dubhe, are moving across the sky in the opposite direction. Therefore, the pattern will eventually become distorted, and the Bear will lose its familiar form. Note that Alkaid appears only slightly less brilliant than Alioth; since it is more than three times as remote from us, it is obviously much more luminous.

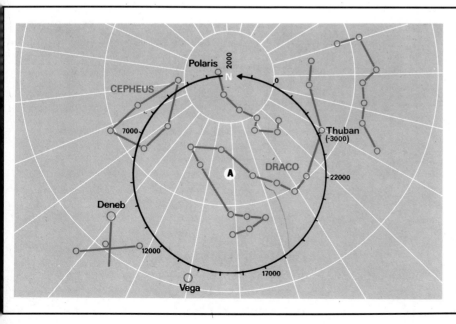

Precession *left* The direction of the Earth's axis, and the position of the celestial pole, are not constant. The Sun and Moon pull on the Earth's equatorial bulge, making the Earth 'wobble', or precess slightly, in the manner of a gyroscope which is starting to topple. It takes 26,000 years for the pole to make one circuit. 5,000 years ago, the pole star was Thuban; in 14,000 years' time it will be Vega.

THE TYPES
OF STARS

Telescopes alone can give us only a limited knowledge of the stars, since no telescope can show a star as anything but a dot of light. We depend mainly upon instruments based upon the principle of the spectroscope which analyze light and enable us to find out what substances are present in the body emitting it.

Light may be regarded as a wave-motion, and the colour of the light depends upon its wavelength. The usual unit is the Ångström (named in honour of the 19th-century Swedish physicist Anders Ångström); one Å is equal to one hundred-millionth part of a centimetre. Visible light ranges from about 7,500 Å (red) down to 3,900 Å (violet).

The science of spectroscopy began with some experiments carried out by Isaac Newton in 1666. Newton passed a beam of sunlight through a glass prism, and found that the light was separated into a rainbow of colours, from red through yellow, green and blue to violet. In the early 19th century the spectrum of the Sun was intensively studied by the German optician Fraunhofer, who found that the rainbow band was crossed by dark lines—now called absorption lines, though sometimes still referred to as Fraunhofer lines. These lines did not change; they always stayed in the same positions, and with the same intensities.

It is now known that an incandescent solid, liquid, or gas at high pressure will yield, by means of a spectroscope, a rainbow or continuous spectrum, whereas a gas at lower pressure will produce discontinuous bright lines. Each line is due to some definite element or group of elements, and these distinctive 'trade-marks' cannot be duplicated; thus two yellow lines in a particular position in the spectrum can be due only to the element sodium. Of course, one element may produce many lines. For instance, iron alone is responsible for thousands.

The bright surface or photosphere of the Sun produces a rainbow spectrum. Above it is the solar atmosphere, made up of rarefied gas; this should produce discrete lines. However, the presence of the continuous spectrum in the background means that these lines appear dark instead of bright. The positions and intensities are unaffected, and so we can tell what elements are present in the Sun. For instance, the two dark lines in the yellow part of the rainbow are due to sodium.

When the spectra of the stars were examined, it was found that they fall into various fairly well-defined types, and each type is given a letter. The original classification had to be revised several times, so that the present-day sequence is alphabetically chaotic; the types are O, B, A, F, G, K, M, R, N and S. Of these, stars of types O, B and A are white or bluish-white; F and G, yellow; K, orange; and the rest orange-red. This indicates a sequence of decreasing temperature, O being the hottest and R, N and S the coolest.

It was natural to assume that this sequence was connected with a star's evolution, and this was supported by the discovery that the stars of 'late' type (K and beyond) were divided into two definite classes: giants and dwarfs. Thus both Betelgeux, in Orion, and the nearest known star, Proxima Centauri, are of type M; but Betelgeux is a huge globe, more than 250 million miles in diameter, with a luminosity thousands of times greater than that of the Sun, whereas Proxima is small and feeble by stellar standards. Red stars of the diameter and luminosity of the Sun seemed not to exist at all. The giant and dwarf classification was less marked for stars of types G and F, and did not apply to the hot stars of 'early' type. Therefore, it was thought that a star began its career as a large, cool red giant, by condensing out of the interstellar material; it then shrank and became hotter, so that at its most luminous it was brilliant white, after which it continued to shrink but also cooled down, ending its career as a dim red dwarf.

These ideas had to be drastically revised when more was learned about the source of stellar energy. A star is not 'burning' in the usual sense of the word;

it is radiating because of nuclear reactions going on inside it. Deep inside the Sun, the temperature is of the order of 14 million degrees Centigrade, and the pressure is tremendous. Hydrogen is very plentiful, and under these conditions the nuclei of hydrogen are combining to form nuclei of the second element in the periodic table, helium. It takes four hydrogen nuclei to make one nucleus of helium, and in the process a little energy is released and a little mass is lost. It is this energy which keeps the Sun shining. The mass-loss amounts to four million tons per second—and yet the Sun is so massive that it will maintain this output and not change appreciably for at least 6,000 million years.

Armed with this information, we can try to draw up a picture of the evolution of a typical star. We still believe that it begins by condensing out of the rarefied interstellar material; as it shrinks, under the influence of gravitation, the interior becomes hot, and when the temperature has become sufficiently high the nuclear reactions can begin. Hydrogen, which is more abundant than all the other elements in the universe put together, is the main 'fuel', and its conversion into helium makes the star radiate steadily for a long period. The rate of evolution depends upon the initial mass; the more massive the star, the quicker it uses up its reserves.

Eventually, however, the supply of available hydrogen begins to run low, and the star has to adjust. The outside layers swell out, and their temperature drops; the core shrinks, and different nuclear reactions begin, with the helium being built up into heavier elements. The star has become a red giant, as Betelgeux is today. Clearly there is a great difference between modern and older theories. Astronomers used to believe that a red giant must be young; we now know that all red giants are well advanced in their stellar life-times.

After various series of reactions, the star approaches a crisis. What happens to it depends upon its mass. With a moderate star, of solar type, the nuclear power fails, and the star collapses into what is called the white dwarf state. The atoms are packed tightly together, with little waste space, and the result is that the star becomes amazingly dense; a thimbleful of white dwarf material would weigh several tons. There is no nuclear energy left, and the star continues to shine very dimly until it becomes a cold, dead globe. White dwarfs are common in the Galaxy (and in other galaxies), though their low luminosities mean that we can study only those which are relatively close to us. The best-known and first-discovered of them is the faint companion of the brilliant Sirius, which is smaller than a planet such as Uranus, but its mass is almost as great as the Sun's. Some of them are much smaller and denser than the companion of Sirius, and there are a few known to us which are considerably smaller than the Earth, though their masses are comparable with that of the Sun. They can even occur in pairs; in 1973 Luyten and Higgins, in the United States, found a double white dwarf, the two revolving components of which are about 550,000 million miles from each other.

If the star is of much greater mass, it may suffer a more spectacular fate, and produce a supernova explosion. Much of the material is blown away into space, and all that remains is an extremely small, super-dense remnant, together with a cloud of expanding gas. Fortunately one of these remnants is conveniently placed for observation, and is 'only' 6,000 light-years away from us. It is known as the Crab Nebula, and is undoubtedly the remains of a supernova which was observed by Chinese and Japanese astronomers in 1054. For a while the supernova shone so brightly that it could be seen with the naked eye in broad daylight.

As well as sending visible light, by which we see it, the Crab Nebula is a source of long-wavelength radiations known as radio waves (though there is no suggestion that they are of artificial origin). Radio telescopes, which are really huge aerials, can focus and study these long radiations. Inside the Crab Nebula there is a radio source which sends out very rapid 'pulses', and is therefore called a pulsar. It has been identified with a very faint star which flashes with the same period, and astronomers now believe that a pulsar is made up of neutrons. A neutron star is far denser than even a white dwarf. Near its centre, a cubic inch of its material would weigh something of the order of 15,000 million tons!

When we consider a star whose initial mass is greater still, we are faced with an extraordinary situation. When the star has exhausted its main store of nuclear energy, and collapses, it continues to do so until it has become so small and so dense that not even light can escape from it. To all intents and purposes, it disappears from the visible universe, and becomes what we call a 'black hole'. Since we cannot observe black holes directly, we can only speculate about them, and though their existence has not been proved, most modern authorities, on recent evidence, believe that they must exist.

The Sun is not massive enough to explode as a supernova, or to become a black hole; it will presumably change into a red giant, and then collapse to the white dwarf condition. During the giant stage it will be 100 times as luminous as it is today, and life on Earth will be destroyed. There is, however, no fear that it will change markedly in output in the foreseeable future.

Variable Stars

Though most stars shine steadily over long periods, some are unstable, and fluctuate over a limited range. Some are regular in behaviour; others are erratic and unpredictable.

The most important variables are undoubtedly the Cepheids—named after the brightest and best-known member of the class, Delta Cephei. They are perfectly regular, and their periods (that is to say, the intervals between successive maxima) are of the order of a few days or weeks. The luminosity of a Cepheid is linked with its period (the longer the period, the more powerful the star),

so that we can estimate the distance of a Cepheid merely by watching it and noting its behaviour. We also have the red long-period stars such as Mira in Cetus, which may sometimes become as bright as Polaris, and has a period of 331 days.

There are many irregular variables; for instance, the U Geminorum or SS Cygni stars undergo periodic outbursts, at intervals of a few weeks, when they brighten by several magnitudes; R Coronæ stars show sudden, erratic falls to minimum, which are spectacular in the range of magnitude the variations can cover.

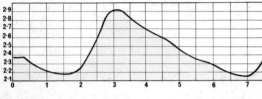

RR Lyræ Variables *left* When we plot the changing magnitude of a variable star against a time-scale, we obtain a light-curve. The light-curve of RR Lyræ has a period of less than a day. Many stars of this type are known, and all seem to have about the same luminosity; they are regular in behaviour. All are too faint to be seen with the naked eye.

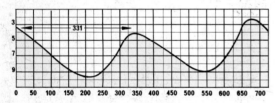

Cepheids *left* This light-curve shows the behaviour of Delta Cephei, which has a period of 5.1 days. It is always bright enough to be seen with the naked eye. Cepheids have periods ranging from 3 days to over 50 days; they are very powerful stars, so that they can be seen across vast distances, and are invaluable as 'standard candles'. They also exist in external galaxies.

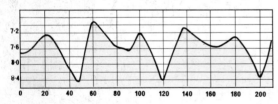

Long-period Variables *left* The light-curve of Mira Ceti, which may exceed the 2nd magnitude, though at minimum it drops to magnitude 9. The average period is 331 days, but there are considerable fluctuations in both period and amplitude, and there is no Cepheid-type relationship between period and luminosity. Like all variables of its kind, Mira is a huge red giant.

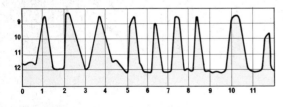

RV Tauri Variables *left* These stars are very luminous, and have light-curves which show alternate deep and shallow minima, though they are to some extent unpredictable and the light-curve is never repeated exactly from one cycle to the next. At times the fluctuations become more or less random. RV Tauri variables are comparatively uncommon.

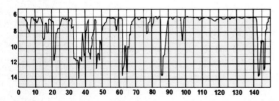

U Geminorum or SS Cygni Variables *left* These are sometimes called 'dwarf novæ'. For most of the time they remain near minimum brightness, with slight fluctuations, but periodically they show outbursts, brightening up by several magnitudes. SS Cygni, whose light-curve is shown here, has a range from magnitude $8\frac{1}{4}$ to $12\frac{1}{2}$; it is the brightest member of the class.

R Coronæ Borealis Variables *left* These stars remain at maximum for most of the time, but suffer sudden, unpredictable falls to minimum. Their spectra show that they are deficient in hydrogen, but very rich in carbon. Very few of them are known. R Coronæ itself is the brightest and best-known; at maximum it is on the fringe of naked-eye visibility.

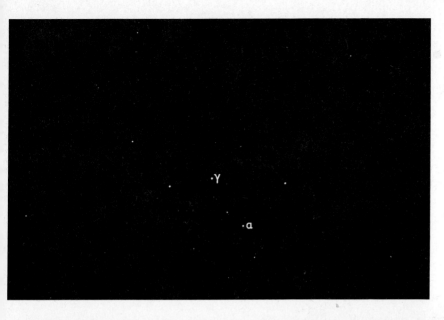

Variable Stars *left*
Cassiopeia is one of the most prominent constellations of the northern skies. Its five chief stars make up a rough W, and of these, two, Gamma and Alpha Cassiopeiæ, are of special interest. Gamma is variable; it has a peculiar spectrum, and is unstable. Generally it is rather fainter than the Pole Star, but at times, as in 1936, it may brighten up to magnitude $1\frac{1}{2}$. Alpha, sometimes known by its old proper name of Shedir, is an orange star of type K, and is thought by some to be variable over a small range (mag. $2\frac{1}{4}$ to $2\frac{1}{2}$); others doubt the variability.

Naked-eye Variable Stars *above* The constellation of Gemini is marked by two bright stars, Castor and Pollux, the Twins. Also in the group are two naked-eye variables; Zeta, a typical Cepheid with a period of 10.2 days, and the semi-regular variable Eta, with a small range and a period of about 230 days.

Double and Multiple Stars

Not all the stars are solitary travellers in space. A surprisingly large number of them are double, made up of two separate components which may be either perfect twins or decidedly unequal in size and luminosity. Double stars whose components are genuinely associated, and are in motion round their common centre of gravity, are known as binaries. Optical doubles, in which the appearance is due to chance alignment with one star almost 'behind' the other, are much less common.

Some double stars are spectacular. A famous case is that of Mizar, the second star in the tail of the Great Bear. With the naked eye a fainter star, Alcor, is easily seen beside Mizar; with a telescope it is found that Mizar itself is double, though the rather unequal components are so close together that with the naked eye they appear as one star.

Multiple systems also occur. For instance, Castor, in Gemini, is made up of two bright components, each of which is itself double; a fainter binary is also associated with the Castor system. Close to Vega is Epsilon Lyræ, which is a naked-eye double; a moderate telescope will again divide each component in two.

It used to be thought that a binary system was the result of the break-up of an originally single star, but this idea has now been generally discarded.

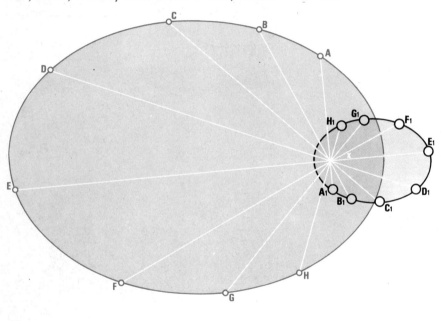

Binary System *left* The two components revolve round the centre of gravity of the system. X represents the centre of gravity of an unequal binary. The more massive component has the smaller orbit (A1, B1 . . . H1), while the less massive component has the larger orbit (A, B . . . H). With equal components, X would be midway between the stars. By studying the orbital movements of a binary, it is possible to work out the combined mass of the system compared with that of the Sun. The periods of binaries range from a day to centuries: the period of the pair Gamma Virginis is 180 years.

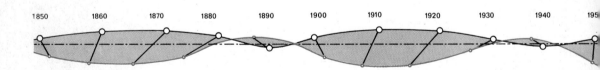

The Sirius pair In 1834, F. Bessel found that Sirius, which has a definite proper motion, was 'weaving its way along', and he deduced the presence of an invisible companion. In 1862 the companion was discovered; it has only one ten-thousandth of the luminosity of its primary, and is now known to be a white dwarf. *Above* The path of Sirius, 1850–1950. *Right* The actual orbital positions in 1930.

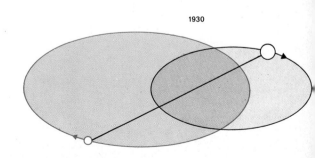

1930

An Optical Double *left* Aldebaran, the red 1st-magnitude star in Taurus (the Bull) has a dim companion of the 11th magnitude. This is not, however, a binary system; the companion is much more remote than Aldebaran itself.

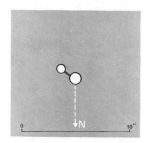

A Rapid Binary *left* Zeta Herculis, which has a period of 34 years. The magnitudes are 3.1 and 5.6; the maximum separation is only 1.6 seconds of arc, so that a fairly powerful telescope is needed to show the system well.

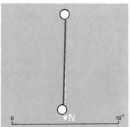

An Equal Double *left* Gamma Arietis, in the constellation of Aries (the Ram). Both components are of magnitude 4.4, and the separation is 8.2 seconds of arc, so that we have a wide pair, easily seen with a small telescope.

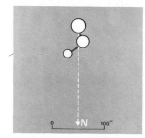

A Triple Star *left* Alpha Centauri, in the far south. This is the nearest of all star-systems. It is made up of a fine binary pair easily seen in a small telescope. The third member of the trio is the faint red dwarf Proxima.

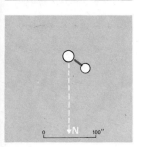

An Unequal Double *left* Albireo or Beta Cygni, where the magnitudes are respectively 3.2 and 5.4. The contrasting colours are spectacular; the primary is golden yellow and very luminous, while the companion is bluish-green.

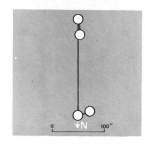

A Multiple Star *left* Epsilon Lyræ, close to the brilliant Vega. The main pair is separable with the naked eye; with a 3-in. telescope, each component is again seen to be double. Several unassociated stars lie in the same telescopic field.

Eclipsing Binaries *below* It sometimes happens that with a binary pair one component may pass in front of the other as seen from the Earth. This means that the total light we receive from the system is reduced, and the star seems to give a long, slow 'wink'. Though it shows apparent fluctuations in light, it is not a genuine variable star; it is an eclipsing binary.

The most famous member of the class is Algol, in the northern constellation of Perseus. Here we have two components, of which the smaller is the hotter and the more luminous. When the brighter component is eclipsed by the fainter (positions 1 and 3, below), Algol fades from magnitude $2\frac{1}{4}$ down to $3\frac{1}{2}$, remaining at minimum for 20 minutes before starting to regain its light. When the fainter component is eclipsed by the brighter (positions 2 and 4) there is a shallow minimum. With Algol, the eclipses are not total; but many eclipsing binaries are known. With Beta Lyræ, near Vega, the components must be almost in contact, and apparent variations in light are always going on.

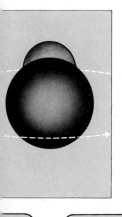

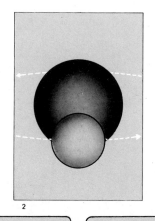

2

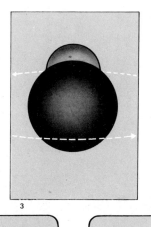

3

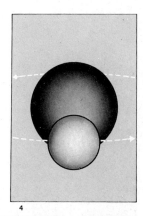

4

Exploding Stars

A nova, or 'temporary star', is not genuinely new. What happens is that a formerly faint star suffers an outburst, and brightens up for a few days or months before returning to its previous obscurity. With an ordinary nova, the outburst affects only the outer layers of the star, and material is ejected, sometimes producing a visible cloud of gas which slowly expands.

Naked-eye novæ have been seen frequently, and some have become brilliant. Such were Nova Persei 1901 and Nova Aquilæ 1918, both of which rivalled the brightest stars in the sky, but have now become extremely faint telescopic objects. Equally interesting, though less spectacular, was the nova in Delphinus (the Dolphin) found by the English amateur astronomer G. E. D. Alcock, in 1967. It reached magnitude $3\frac{1}{2}$, and remained visible to the naked eye for months; before its outburst it was of the 12th magnitude. It is 30,000 light-years away, so that we have been watching the results of an outburst which occurred 30,000 years ago.

Nova DQ Herculis, 1934 *below* This nova was discovered by an English amateur, J. Prentice, and attained the 1st magnitude; its light-curve for 1934–5 is shown below. The photographs *below left*, taken in 1951, show that the nova is now a close binary system associated with nebulosity. Nothing is known of its pre-outburst spectral type.

Nova HR Dephini, 1967 *below* This was one of the 'slowest' of all modern novæ, and in 1973, six years after its outburst, it was still bright enough to be seen with a small telescope. Before it became a nova, it was an O-type star of magnitude 12. This was Alcock's first nova discovery, but he has since found two more—to say nothing of four comets!

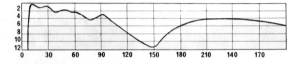

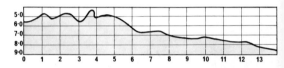

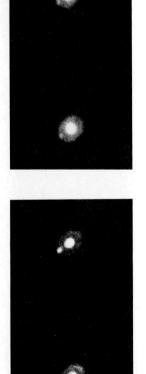

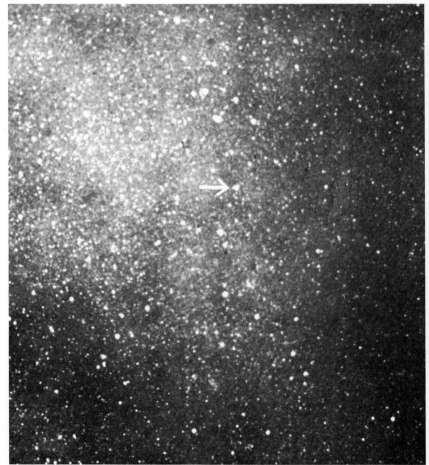

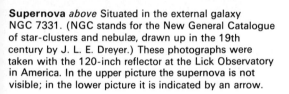

Supernova *above*. Situated in the external galaxy NGC 7331. (NGC stands for the New General Catalogue of star-clusters and nebulæ, drawn up in the 19th century by J. L. E. Dreyer.) These photographs were taken with the 120-inch reflector at the Lick Observatory in America. In the upper picture the supernova is not visible; in the lower picture it is indicated by an arrow.

Supernova *above*. Situated in the external galaxy NGC 4725. This galaxy is a spiral in the northern constellation of Coma Berenices. The supernova is shown only on the second photograph, and is indicated by the arrow. At maximum, a supernova may shine as brilliantly as all the other stars in its galaxy combined, but the outburst is over after a period of a few weeks.

Supernovæ in External Galaxies

Only four supernovæ have been seen in our own Galaxy during the past thousand years. These were the stars of 1006 (in Lupus); 1054 (in Taurus; the Crab Nebula supernova); 1572 (Tycho's Star, in Cassiopeia); and 1604 (Kepler's Star, in Ophiuchus). None has been seen since the invention of the telescope, and so astronomers are reduced to studying the supernovæ which can be seen in outer galaxies. Many of these have been found, of which the most spectacular was the 1885 star in the Andromeda Spiral; this supernova reached the 6th magnitude, just visible with the naked eye, but its nature was not then appreciated.

All the four known supernovæ in our Galaxy are present-day radio sources, and it is likely that all of them have produced pulsars, though only that in the Crab Nebula has been identified.

Bright Novæ

Year and Constellation	Maximum magnitude	Discoverer	Notes
1572 Cassiopeia	−4	Tycho Brahe	Tycho's Star. Now a radio source. Supernova.
1600 Cygnus	3	Blaeu	P Cygni; shell star; now variable between mag. 4½ and 5¼.
1604 Ophiuchus	−2.3	?	Kepler's Star; supernova.
1670 Vulpecula	3	Anthelm	Not now identifiable.
1783 Sagitta	6	D'Agelet	
1848 Ophiuchus	4	Hind	
1866 Corona Borealis	2	Birmingham	T Coronæ; recurrent nova; second outburst in 1946.
1876 Cygnus	3	Schmidt	Q Cygni.
1891 Auriga	4.2	Anderson	
1898 Sagittarius	4.9	Fleming	
1901 Perseus	0.0	Anderson	GK Persei. Close binary.
1903 Gemini	5.0	Turner	
1910 Ara	6.0	Fleming	
1910 Lacerta	4.6	Espin	
1912 Gemini	3.3	Enebo	
1918 Aquila	−1.1	Bower	Now a close binary.
1918 Monoceros	5.7	Wolf	
1920 Cygnus	2.0	Denning	
1925 Pictor	2.0	Watson	RR Pictoris. Fine slow nova. Now a close binary.

Year and Constellation	Maximum magnitude	Discoverer	Notes
1927 Taurus	6.0	Schwassman & Wachmann	
1934 Hercules	1.2	Prentice	DQ Herculis. Fine slow nova. Now a close binary.
1936 Aquila	5.4	Tamm	
1936 Lacerta	1.9	Gomi	CP Lacertæ. Fast nova; rapid decline.
1936 Sagittarius	4.5	Okayabasi	
1939 Monoceros	4.3	Whipple & Wachmann	
1942 Puppis	0.4	Dawson	Fast nova.
1950 Lacerta	6.0	Bertaud	
1960 Hercules	5.0	Hassell	
1963 Hercules	5.7	Hassell	HR Delphini. Exceptionally slow nova. Pre-outburst mag. 12.
1967 Delphinus	3.7	Alcock	
1968 Vulpecula	4.3	Alcock	Fast nova; mag. 12 at end of 1969.
1970 Serpens	4.6	Honda	
1970 Aquila	6	Honda	

The supernova S Andromedæ (1885) in the Andromeda Galaxy, M.31, was just visible with the naked eye when at maximum.

Nebulae

By no means all of the material in the Galaxy is contained in the stars. There is also a tremendous amount of interstellar matter, and, in particular, the cloudy objects which we call nebulæ.

A nebula is made up of extremely tenuous gas, together with 'dust'. The best-known example is the Great Nebula in Orion, M.42, which lies close to the Hunter's Belt. It is clearly visible with the naked eye, even though it is 1,500 light-years from us, and it is very extensive; but as has been pointed out by D. A. Allen, a 'core sample one inch in diameter drilled through the entire nebula would collect only the weight of one new penny'.

Some nebulæ shine only by reflecting the light of stars contained in them, but others, containing extremely hot stars, are 'excited', and emit a certain amount of light on their own account. Gaseous or galactic nebulæ are of special interest to astronomers because it seems that they are stellar birthplaces; inside them, fresh stars are being produced out of the nebular material. In the remote past, over 5,000 million years ago, our Sun was doubtless produced in very much the same way.

There are many nebulæ in our Galaxy, and we can also see them in external systems millions of light-years away.

(The 'M' in M.42 stands for 'Messier', and refers to the catalogue of nebular objects drawn up in 1781 by the French astronomer Charles Messier.)

Distribution of Galactic Nebulæ *below* In this map, the galactic poles are at the top and bottom, with the galactic plane running across the centre. The nebulæ tend to be commonest near the main plane, and there are virtually none near the galactic poles.

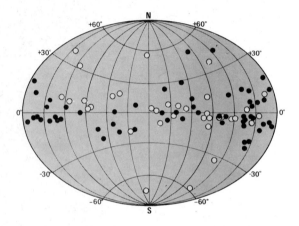

An Emission Nebula *below* If a nebula is illuminated by a very hot star, it can be excited to self-luminosity. In the diagram the star concerned is shown at A; the light reaching the Earth (B) is characteristic of the substances making up the nebula. A nebulous region which is excited to luminosity in this way is called an H-II region, since hydrogen (H) is the most abundant element. The photograph is of M.8, the Lagoon Nebula in Sagittarius, which is a typical emission nebula. It is 4,850 light-years away; the lagoon effect is produced by foreground dust-clouds. M.8 is visible with a small telescope, though its structure cannot be examined without photographs taken with large instruments.

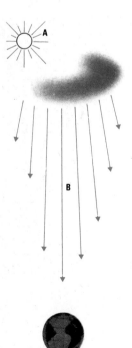

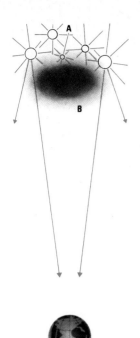

A Dark Nebula *above* When Sir William Herschel, the great observer of the late 18th century, was examining the sky, he came across some starless patches which he called 'holes in the heavens'. In fact these patches are not holes; they are dark nebulæ. There is no essential difference between a bright nebula and a dark one; it all depends on whether there are any suitable stars to provide illumination. In the diagram, the nebula B cuts off the light of the stars beyond (A). The most celebrated dark nebula is the Coal Sack in the Southern Cross. The photograph to the right shows dark nebulosity in Monoceros (the Unicorn). The few stars seen against the dark mass are, of course, in the foreground.

Reflection Nebula *below* With some nebulæ, the star producing the illumination is not hot enough to make the nebulosity shine by its own light and the result is a pure reflection nebula. In the diagram, the star A is lighting up the nebulosity.

The most famous reflection nebula is probably that in the Pleiades cluster. The photograph to the right shows the neighbourhood of the star Merope, one of the Seven Sisters. The nebulosity in the cluster is extensive, but is hard to see by ordinary direct observation; photographic methods are needed. The fact that there is so much nebulosity confirms that the Pleiades cluster is comparatively young by cosmic standards.

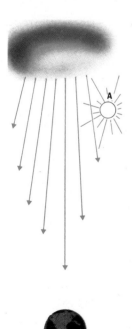

Star Clusters and Interstellar Matter

Among the most spectacular objects in the sky are the open or loose star-clusters, some of which are visible with the naked eye. Some are large and rich, while others are so poorly defined that they may not form a true cluster but may be merely a chance aggregation.

Pride of place must go to the Pleiades (M.45), in Taurus. At a casual glance it looks like a haze, but closer inspection will show individual stars in it; the brightest is Alcyone, of the 3rd magnitude. Anyone with good eyes should see seven or eight stars in the cluster on a clear night. It has been calculated that 300 to 500 stars are contained in a spherical area 50 light-years in diameter; there is also extensive reflection nebulosity.

Also in Taurus we find the Hyades, round the bright red star Aldebaran. The Hyades are more scattered than the Pleiades, and are overpowered by the light of Aldebaran—which does not really belong to the cluster at all, but lies midway between the Hyades and ourselves. Other famous clusters are Præsepe, or the Beehive, in Cancer, the Sword-Handle, in Perseus (where we have two clusters side by side), and the Jewel Box, in the Southern Cross. Many thousands of loose clusters are known, both in our Galaxy and in external systems.

The stars in any particular cluster are of comparable age; if the leaders are hot and white we may assume that the cluster is young; if they are yellow or red giants, the cluster is older.

An open cluster cannot be regarded as a stable system; over a sufficiently long period of time it will be disrupted by the gravitational effects of non-cluster stars, and will lose its separate identity.

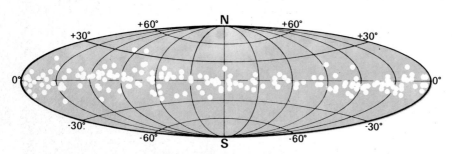

Distribution of Galactic Clusters *left*
Since most of the open or loose clusters are relatively young, they lie not far from the main plane of the Galaxy. A few exceptional clusters, apparently older, lie farther from the plane; such is M.67, in Cancer.

Globular Cluster *left*
This is quite different from an open cluster. It is much more symmetrical, and much richer. M.5, in Serpens, shown in the photograph, is a typical globular cluster, 27,000 light-years away from us and 130 light-years in diameter. More than 100 globulars are known in our Galaxy; they lie around the edges of the main system, and have been described as an 'outer framework'. They contain little interstellar material, so they are presumably old; star formation inside them has ceased. Only three are visible with the naked eye; M.13, in Herculis, and two more in the far south, Omega Centauri and 47 Tucanæ.

Bright and Dark Nebulosity *above* Near the star
Gamma Cygni, this is one of the rich regions of the
Milky Way, but it also contains the celebrated rifts, well
shown in the photograph, which are due to dark
obscuring matter. The photograph was taken with the
48-inch Schmidt telescope at Palomar, U.S.A.

THE GALAXIES

When Messier drew up his catalogue of nebulous objects, he made no distinction between the various types, although he was aware that there were tremendous differences between nebulæ and clusters. It also seemed that there were two kinds of nebulæ; some could be resolved into stars, while others could not. In 1845 the Earl of Rosse, using the great 72-inch reflecting telescope that he built himself, discovered that many of the resolvable or starry nebulæ were spiral in form, like catherine-wheels. Inevitably, it was suggested that the starry nebulæ might be independent systems, far beyond our own.

This had been proposed by Sir William Herschel, though at the time when Herschel was observing (the last few decades of the 18th century and the early years of the 19th) no proof could be obtained. Neither could Lord Rosse clear the matter up, and the idea fell into disfavour.

Then came the discovery of the Cepheid period-luminosity law. As we have noted, the real luminosity of a Cepheid depends upon the way in which it fluctuates; the longer the period, the more powerful the star. Cepheids can be seen in some of the resolvable nebulæ, notably in the Andromeda Spiral, which is the brightest of them; and in 1923 E. E. Hubble, using the 100-inch reflector at Mount Wilson, made the fundamental breakthrough by measuring the distances of Cepheids in the Andromeda Spiral. His results were conclusive: the Spiral was very remote indeed, and was a galaxy in its own right. We now know that its distance from us is 2.2 million light-years, and that it is considerably larger than the Galaxy in which we live.

Once this had been established, other galaxies were studied in the same way. They were found to contain objects of all kinds, including open clusters, gaseous nebulæ, and supergiant stars; even supernovæ have been observed in them. Of course, only the nearer galaxies could be examined in detail. The more remote systems look like faint blurs of light in the sky, and we have to use indirect methods to find out how far away they are.

The distribution of the galaxies in space is not uniform. They tend to occur in clusters or groups, and we live in one such assemblage, known as the Local Group; as well as our Galaxy, it includes the Andromeda Spiral, the smaller spiral in Triangulum, the two Clouds of Magellan in the southern hemisphere, and more than two dozen smaller systems, most of which are elliptical in form, although some are irregular. Other known clusters of galaxies are much richer. The cluster in the constellation of Virgo contains hundreds of members, some of which are true giants. (Note that there is no similarity between an open or globular star-cluster, and a cluster of galaxies.)

Spectroscopic methods have shown that apart from the members of our Local Group, all the galaxies are receding from us, and that the universe is in a state of expansion. The spectrum of a galaxy is made up of the combined spectra of the stars contained in it; the main spectral lines can be recognized, and are shifted to the long-wave or red end, which indicates that the light-sources are moving away from us. The speed of recession increases with distance, and we know of galaxies which are racing away at appreciable fractions of the speed of light. Our estimates of their distances depend entirely on the red shifts in their spectra, assuming that we interpret the spectral red shifts as Doppler effects. A few authorities question this; if it were eventually proved that the red shifts are due to some other cause, theories would have to be extensively revised once again. Meanwhile, the concept of an expanding universe is still very much in vogue.

Not many galaxies are visible with the naked eye, or with modest telescopes. In the far south the two Clouds of Magellan are very prominent; they are irregular in form, and have been regarded as satellite galaxies associated with our own much more massive Galaxy. They are relatively close, 180,000 light-years from us, and so we can study them in detail. North of the celestial equator, only the Andromeda Spiral, M.31, is visible without optical aid—and then only when its position is known. Seen through a small or even a moderately large telescope, it is rather a disappointing object, though photographs bring out its structure and show that it is a spiral lying at an angle to us. Not far away from it in the sky is M.33, the Triangulum Spiral, which is much fainter. Binoculars will show it, and a few people with exceptional sight claim to have glimpsed it with the naked eye, but it is much less condensed than the Andromeda Spiral.

Although Messier's catalogue contains more than two dozen galaxies, most of them are too faint to be seen with amateur equipment, except as vague patches. This is only to be expected, because of their tremendous distances from us. It is always interesting to take a small telescope and search for galaxies—but do not expect to see any brilliant spiral objects!

When radio astronomy became an important branch of research, after the end of the Second World War, it was found that some galaxies were strangely powerful sources of radio waves. Such is M.87, a giant elliptical galaxy in Virgo, which is about 41 million light-years from us, and has a curious jet of luminous material issuing from it. In addition, M.87 is also a source of X-rays and is presumably very active. Another strong radio source is the irregular galaxy M.82, in Ursa Major, which is much closer (only $8\frac{1}{2}$ million light-years away). There are gaseous filaments to be seen which are expanding outward from the centre of the system at immense speeds of up to 625 miles per second, and appear to indicate that a gigantic explosion took place in the galactic nucleus more than a million years ago.

Another radio galaxy is Centaurus A, too far south to be seen from Europe. This looks like a compound system, and some years ago it was believed that the radio emissions from it and the other galaxies of its kind were due to collisions. According to this theory, two galaxies belonging to the same group could collide, and pass through each other rather in the manner of two orderly crowds moving in opposite directions. The individual stars would seldom hit each other, but the material spread between them would be in collision all the time, producing the radio energy which we can pick up.

The theory seemed plausible, but it was then found to have fatal weaknesses. In particular, collision could not produce nearly so much radio energy as we actually receive. The concept of colliding galaxies was given up, but at the moment we have to admit that the reason for the strong emissions at radio wavelengths remains rather a mystery.

Even more enigmatical are the quasars. They look almost stellar in appearance, and indeed for many years they were overlooked, since they were taken to be ordinary stars. They were tracked down because of their strong radio emissions; and when their optical spectra were examined, they were found to be receding at immense velocities, It followed that they must be very remote. In 1973 a quasar was discovered with a recessional velocity of over 90 per cent of the velocity of light. To add to the puzzle, some of the quasars vary in output over short periods, indicating that they must be much smaller than galaxies—even though they are so luminous. It has been estimated that a powerful quasar can shine as brilliantly, by producing as much energy, as 200 average galaxies put together. As with the ordinary galaxies, estimates of the distances of quasars are based upon the red shifts in their spectra. Were these shifts not Doppler effects there would be no need to assume that the quasars are so remote and luminous as most astronomers think.

If the quasars are so powerful, what gives them their energy? Here again we have to admit that we are uncertain. Neither do we know whether a quasar and a radio galaxy represent different stages in the evolution of the same class of object.

One fascinating theory has been proposed by the Swedish astronomer Hannes Alfvén, who believes that some of the galaxies may be composed of anti-matter—that is to say, matter with properties the exact opposite of those making up the Earth and ourselves. A meeting between anti-matter and ordinary matter would result in mutual annihilation and the release of energy. It could be, then, that a quasar is a place where this mutual annihilation is going on. Unfortunately it seems that proof or denial of this interesting idea will be very difficult to obtain. In any case, quasars are undoubtedly of tremendous cosmological significance. They were identified only in 1963, and have been intensively studied ever since. However, we still do not know their true nature.

How many galaxies are there? All we can say with certainty is that the world's most powerful telescopes are capable of photographing about 1,000 million of them, and this represents only part of the total. Some are clearly larger than our own system, while others are smaller; they are of various forms, and some of them have special characteristics, such as unusual energy at radio wavelengths. If the law of 'the further, the faster' holds good, then a galaxy which is sufficiently far away will be receding at the velocity of light, and will pass beyond the edge of the observable universe; in this case we can have no clue as to how many galaxies exist in regions forever hidden from us. Neither can we tell whether space is limited in extent, or whether it is infinite. Only by continuing to study the most remote objects available for our inspection can we hope to learn more about these fundamental problems.

Mapping the Galaxies

The stars in the Milky Way are not genuinely crowded together; they simply lie in almost the same line of sight, and the milky appearance is due to our looking along the main plane of the flattened Galaxy. The map of the Milky Way given here was drawn by Martin and Tatiana Tesküla at the Lund Observatory, Sweden. The co-ordinates refer to galactic latitude and longitude, measured from the mean plane of the Milky Way; the zero point for longitude is the intersection between the galactic plane and the celestial equator, on the borders of Aquila and Serpens. The north galactic pole lies in Coma Berenices, and the south galactic pole in Sculptor. Both these areas are very poor in bright stars, though rich in galaxies. Conversely, galaxies cannot be seen near the Milky Way plane, because they are hidden by the galactic dust and gas.

Various well-known stars are shown on the Swedish map, but the positions are rather distorted, because the map has had to be drawn on an unusual projection.

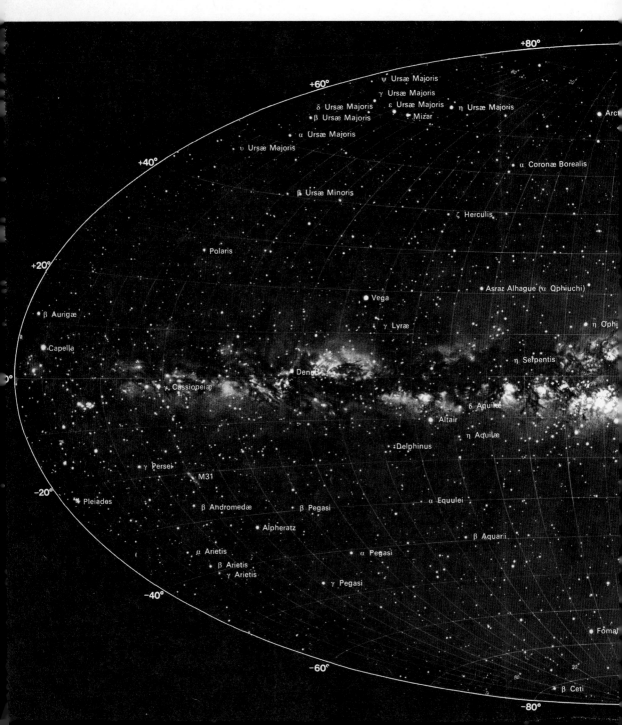

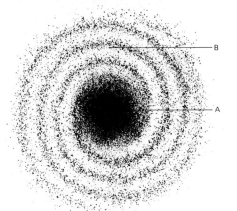

The Milky Way *left, below* It is instructive to compare the Swedish map of the Milky Way with a 'bird's-eye view', shown to the left. The Galaxy is a spiral, 100,000 light-years in diameter; the Sun (B) lies some 32,000 light-years from the centre (A). We cannot see the spiral arms directly, because we are living in the midst of the system not far from the edge of an arm.

Types of Galaxies

It would be quite wrong to assume that all external systems are spiral. For example, the two closest of the bright galaxies—the Clouds of Magellan—are irregular in form. Other galaxies are elliptical or spherical, and even with the spirals we have many dissimilarities in form.

We must also remember that appearances can be deceptive. Some of the spirals are almost edge-on to us, so that we cannot appreciate them fully; unfortunately this is so with the Andromeda Spiral, which lies at an inconvenient angle. Were it face-on, as is the Whirlpool Galaxy, M.51, in Canes Venatici, it would appear much more imposing than it actually does. With very distant galaxies, it is naturally impossible to decide whether they are spiral, elliptical or globular; there is a limit to what can be learned from a tiny blur on a photographic plate.

Our Galaxy is a typical spiral—apart from the fact that it may be rather above the average in size and mass. We cannot see its form, simply because we live inside it.

Galaxies such as our own are in rotation, and with the spirals it has been established that the arms are trailing. We have much less information about some of the other types. Of special interest are the Seyfert galaxies, which have bright, condensed nuclei and inconspicuous spiral arms; many of them are strong radio emitters, and it has been suggested (albeit tentatively) that there may be a close link between Seyfert galaxies and quasars.

There has been much discussion about the evolutionary sequence of a typical galaxy. Does a spiral turn into an elliptical system, or vice versa? It is tempting to suggest that any normal galaxy goes through both a spiral and an elliptical stage, and if so we must assume that the spiral period is the earlier of the two; this is because a spiral contains a great deal of interstellar material, and its leading stars are hot and white, whereas in an elliptical system the main stars have already evolved off the Main Sequence and much of the star-forming material has been used up. (This is admittedly a gross over-simplification of the situation, but the principle is valid.) Unfortunately there are various objections; the elliptical galaxies appear in general to be much more massive than the spirals, and there are theoretical difficulties as well.

At the moment we have to confess that we are almost totally ignorant of the life-story of a galaxy, and it is unsafe to claim that one type of galaxy may evolve into another. Neither do we know how or why the spiral arms form, or whether they are permanent features in a system which develops them.

Elliptical Galaxies *above* Classed from EO (globular) to E7 (very elliptical). M.87, in Virgo, is a giant system of type E0, and a strong radio source.

A Spiral Galaxy *above* NGC 7217 Pegasi: type Sa. The nucleus is well-defined, and the spiral arms are symmetrical and tightly-wound. The nucleus is the most brilliant part.

'Barred' Spirals *above* Some spirals have 'bars' through their nuclei; classed as SBa, SBb and SBc. This galaxy, NGC 3504, in Leo Minor, is SBa. Large nucleus, tight spiral arms.

An E4 Galaxy *above* Dwarf system
NGC 147 in Cassiopeia. Typical of the
small systems. The leading stars have
evolved off the Main Sequence, and
star formation has virtually ceased.

NGC 205, an E6 Galaxy *above* One
of the two small companions of the
Andromeda Spiral. It has no definite
structure, is relatively small, and
contains little interstellar material.

M.81 Ursæ Majoris *above*
Sb-type spiral with arms more
developed than those of NGC 7217.
Like the irregular galaxy M.82, it is a
radio source of unusual power.

Triangulum Spiral, M.33 *above*
Sc-type system, with a nucleus less
well-defined with less pronounced
spiral arms than Sa or Sb types. More
distant than the Andromeda Spiral.

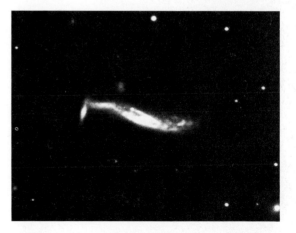

An SBb Galaxy *above* NGC 7479
in Pegasus. The bar formation is more
evident, and there are only two
noticeable arms, which extend from
the ends of the bar.

An SBc Galaxy *above* In Hercules.
The bar formation is dominant, and
the arms are reduced to little more
than extensions of it. The reason for
the formation of bars is not known.

THE STAR MAPS

The first star maps and catalogues were drawn up many centuries ago, and Ptolemy of Alexandria, who died around A.D. 180, listed 48 constellations —all of which are still to be found on modern maps, though not in precisely the form as given by Ptolemy. Nowadays 88 constellations are recognized; some, such as Orion and Ursa Major, are large and brilliant, while others, such as Leo Minor and Microscopium, are so small and ill-defined that they do not seem to merit individual names. Sir John Herschel, son of the discoverer of Uranus, once commented that the constellation patterns seemed to have been drawn up so as to cause the maximum possible confusion and inconvenience. This is probably true, but they have become so well-established that there is no prospect of altering them now.

The constellation names range from the mythological (Cepheus, Cassiopeia, Perseus) to the commonplace (Telescopium, Microscopium, Sextans). In 1603 the German astronomer Bayer allotted each star a Greek letter, beginning with Alpha and ending with Omega; thus ideally the brightest star in, say, Orion should be lettered Alpha Orionis, the second Beta, and so on. In practice the sequence is often not followed (in Orion Beta, or Rigel, is brighter than Alpha, or Betelgeux) and of course only 24 stars can be lettered in each constellation. The Greek letters are given on the maps in the following pages; numbers are those given by John Flamsteed in his famous star-catalogue drawn up, on the orders of Charles II, at Greenwich Observatory.

Originally all the bright stars were given proper names. A few of these come from the Greek (Sirius, for instance, which comes from the Greek word for sparkling), but most are Arabic. Some of the names were strange; for instance the three leading stars in the obscure constellation of Libra (the Scales of Balance) were called Zubenelgenubi, Zubenelchemali and Zubenelhakrabi. A few of the names are more modern; thus the two brightest stars in Delphinus (the Dolphin) were named Svalocin and Rotanev. The names were given by one Nicolaus Venator, for reasons which must be rather obvious. Today the proper names of the stars are seldom used, except for the brightest two dozen stars in the sky.

Clusters and nebulæ are indicated by the NGC or New General Catalogue numbers; if the object is included in Messier's catalogue, the M number is added in brackets.

On any map it is vitally important to give a reliable scale of magnitudes. The only way to do so is to make the stars different sizes—though it is an unsatisfactory method since no star, however bright, appears as more than a point (with the obvious exception of the Sun). The diagram on page 33 shows the scale adopted here. Generally, anyone with keen eyes can see stars down to magnitude 6 on a clear, moonless night; under exceptional conditions it may be possible to see down to 6½. The maps in this book are complete for all the prominent naked-eye stars.

There is also the question of colour, which in turn is linked with the star's surface temperature and spectral type. As we have seen, there is a definite spectral sequence which is based on decreasing surface temperature (though it is not an evolutionary sequence, as used to be supposed). Most of the stars are contained in types B, A, F, G, K and M, of which the first two are white, the second two yellow, and the last two orange or red.

The right-hand diagram shows the situation clearly. With a hot star, the maximum intensity of radiation will be in the comparatively short wavelength range, and so the star will appear bluish or white; with lower temperature, the maximum radiation will become longer, and so the star will look redder. Nowadays we know of stars which radiate entirely in the infra-red, so that optically they cannot be seen at all; it has been suggested that these are very young stars, still contracting toward the Main Sequence and in which nuclear reactions have not begun—though on this point there is no universal agreement, and different authorities hold different opinions.

In the maps, an attempt has been made to

show the main star-colours. For instance Betel-geux and Antares, which are of spectral type M, are given as red; and indeed their hues are obvious with the naked eye. Yet with fainter stars the colours do not show up without optical aid, simply because the intensity of the light is too low. To see the colours properly, use binoculars or a wide-field telescope. Many of the more obviously-coloured stars are tinted in the charts. One example is Dubhe, in Ursa Major, which is the brighter of the two pointers to the Pole Star. Its spectral type is K, and to the naked eye it will probably appear white, but—as the map indicates —it is an orange star, as a glance through binocu-lars will show.

Variable and double stars are also indicated, as shown in the key. The positions of some novæ are given, though virtually all of these are now extremely faint telescopic objects.

On these maps, each hemisphere of the sky has been divided into four quarters. This means that the relationship between the various parts of the sky is clearly shown; but the method has its disadvantages also, because inevitably some well-marked patterns are inconveniently chopped up. The celestial equator runs right through Orion, passing very close to Mintaka or Delta Orionis in the Hunter's Belt; thus Betelgeux is in the northern hemisphere of the sky and Rigel in the southern, so that they appear on different maps.

The declination of the equator is o degrees, and on these maps the equator runs round the periphery of the chart, so that declination 90 degrees lies at the centre of the full circle. The numbers around the edge of the maps indicate hours of right ascension, which is measured from the First Point of Aries, or vernal equinox—the point where the ecliptic cuts the celestial equator.

As can be seen from the map, the equinox now lies in Pisces; this is the result of precession.

Looking at a map of the night sky may tend to give the impression that learning one's way around is a difficult matter. Yet nothing could be further from the truth. Once a constellation has been identified, it will not easily be forgotten; most of the main groups are distinctive, and the most prominent constellations may be used as direction-finders for locating the rest. For in-stance, the best way to find the brilliant orange Arcturus, in Boötes (the Herdsman) is to follow round the line of stars making up the tail of the Great Bear; this line will lead straight to Arcturus —and if continued still further it will show the way to Spica, in the southern hemisphere of the sky. A little practice will work wonders, and any-one who takes the trouble to spend half an hour or so outdoors under a clear sky for several con-secutive nights will soon find that he can tell one group from another.

The whole of the sky is shown on these maps. Of course, an observer in one hemisphere will have a 'reverse' view of the opposite hemisphere. Compared with an observer in the northern hemisphere, a southern observer will see Regulus at the top of the Sickle of Leo instead of at the bottom. However, one soon adapts.

It is impossible to show the positions of the planets on permanent star-maps, because the planets wander about. However, they keep to the well-defined band of the Zodiac, which includes 12 constellations: Aries, Taurus, Gemini, Cancer, Leo, Virgo, Libra, Scorpio, Sagittarius, Capri-cornus, Aquarius and Pisces. Should you find a bright object in one of these groups, and cannot locate it on the map, you may be sure that it is a planet.

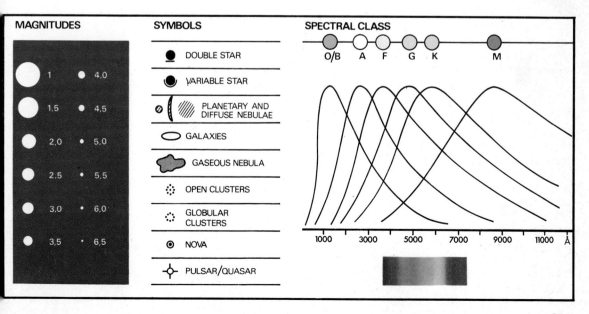

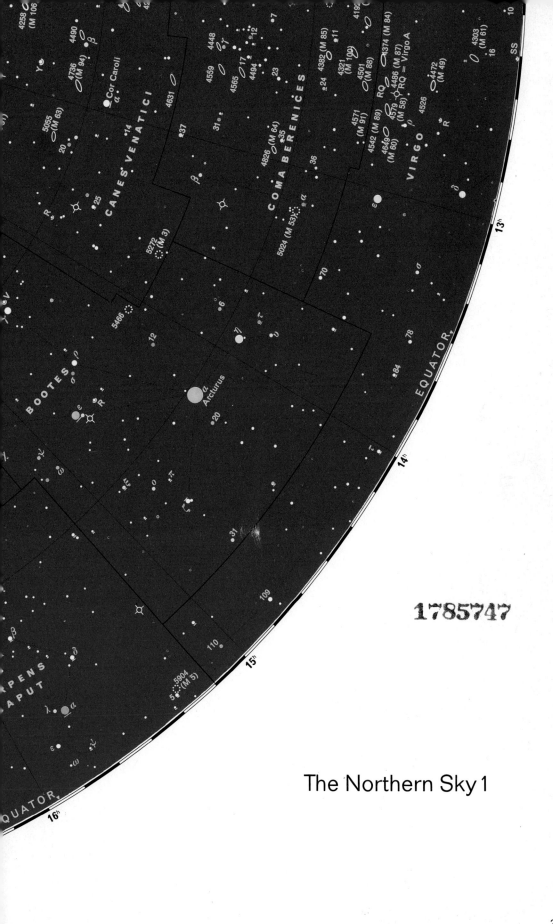

The Northern Sky 1

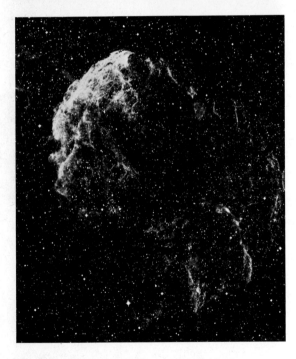

The Spiral Galaxy M.94 *top* Situated in Canes Venatici (the Hunting Dogs). It is intermediate in type between Sa and Sb, and is over 32 million light-years away. M.94 lies near the star Cor Caroli, or Alpha Canum Venaticorum; it is of magnitude $8\frac{1}{2}$, and small telescopes can do no more than show it as a blur.

Gaseous Nebula IC 443 *above* Situated in Gemini. This is by no means bright, and is beyond the range of small telescopes. It may well be a supernova remnant.

The Globular Cluster M.13 *above* Situated in Hercules. This is the finest globular in the northern hemisphere; it is just visible with the naked eye when the sky iş dark and clear, and may be found about one-third of the way from Eta to Zeta Herculis. It is 22,500 light-years away, and 100 light-years in diameter. It is a splendid sight in a moderate telescope, because the outer parts of it are not difficult to resolve into stars. The only globular clusters which surpass it are Omega Centauri and 47 Tucanæ, in the far south of the sky, never visible from Europe.

M.51, the Whirlpool Galaxy *above* Situated in Canes
Venatici. It is of the 8th magnitude, so that small
telescopes will show it, but of course photographs are
needed to reveal its spiral form. It was actually the first
galaxy to be recognized as a spiral (by Lord Rosse, in
1845); it is excellently displayed, since it is face-on to
us. Its distance from us is 37 million light-years.

The Northern Sky 2

The Northern Sky 2

The Irregular Galaxy M.82 *below* Situated in Ursa Major. It is notable as being a very strong radio source, and the movements of the gaseous filaments indicate that a tremendous explosion took place inside it about 1½ million years before our current view of it; of course our information is out of date, because M.82 is 10 million light-years away. It is adjacent to a considerably brighter galaxy, the spiral M.81, which also is a radio source.

Loose Spiral galaxy, NGC 2403 *bottom left* Situated in the very obscure constellation of Camelopardalis. The nucleus is very ill defined, and the spiral arms are not sufficiently well developed to be symmetrical, so that the galaxy is classed as being of type Sc. It is of only the 9th magnitude, so that it cannot be well seen in a small telescope; the surface brightness is low. This photograph was taken with the 200-in. reflector at Palomar, U.S.A.

The Open Spiral M.101 *bottom right* Situated in Ursa Major. It is of magnitude 9½, so that it is comparatively faint; it is, however, one of the closer spirals, at 'only' 11.5 million light-years from us, and is considerably smaller than our Galaxy. Because it is diffuse, it is not particularly easy to locate. In 1909 a supernova was seen in it.

The Rosette Nebula, NGC 2237 *below* Situated in Monoceros. The Rosette Nebula is gaseous, and is a member of our Galaxy; it is a typical emission nebula. The photograph shows it strikingly, but it must be remembered that the red colour is too faint to be seen visually. Look at the nebula, even through a very powerful telescope, and it will appear white. The photograph was taken with the 200-in. reflector at Palomar, U.S.A.

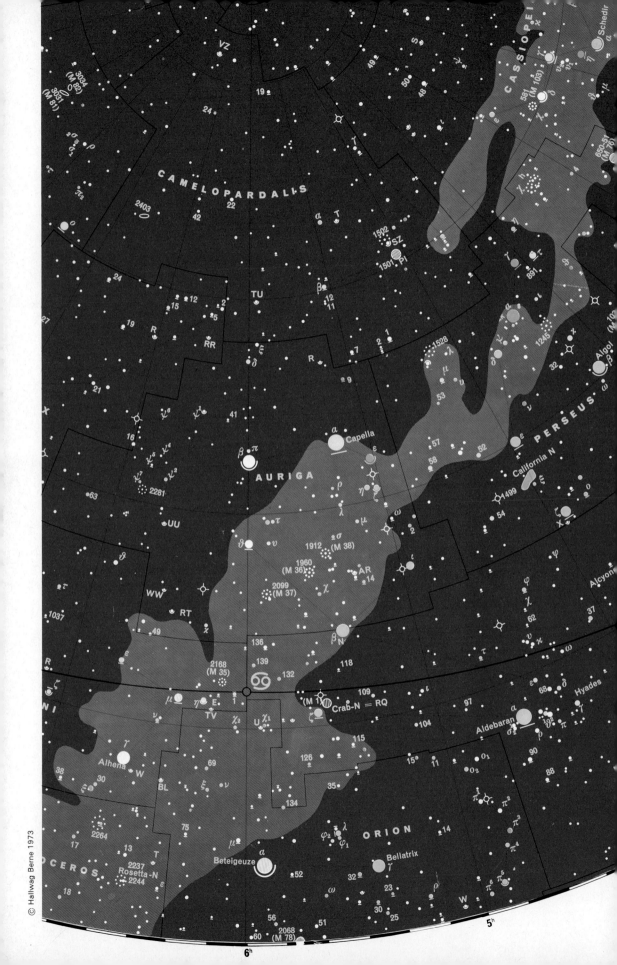

The Northern Sky 3

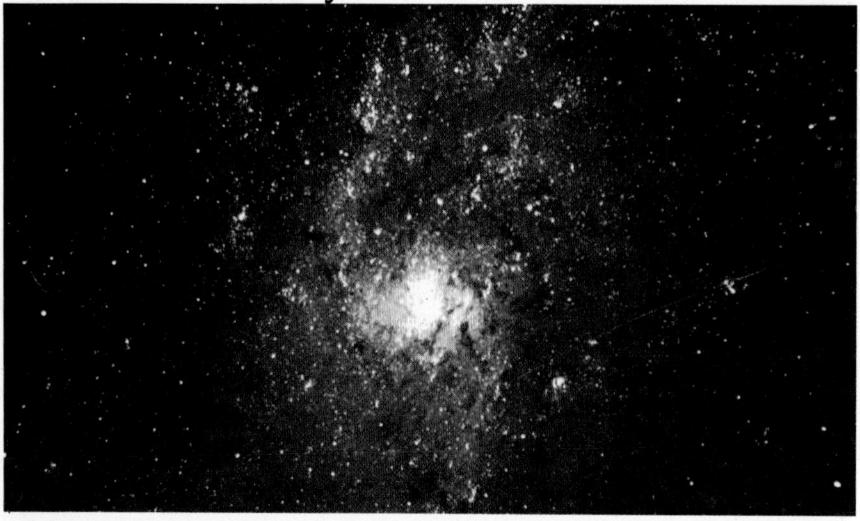

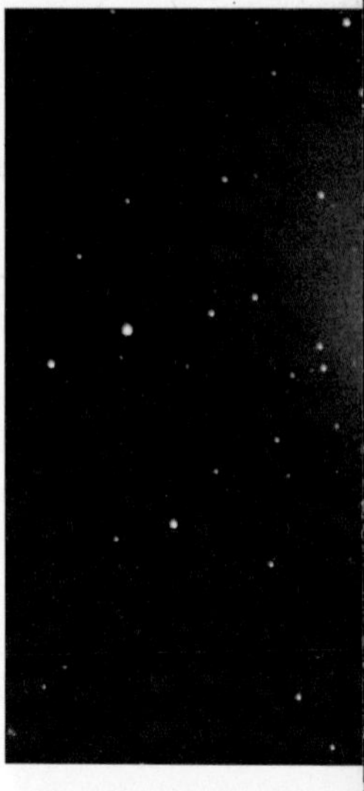

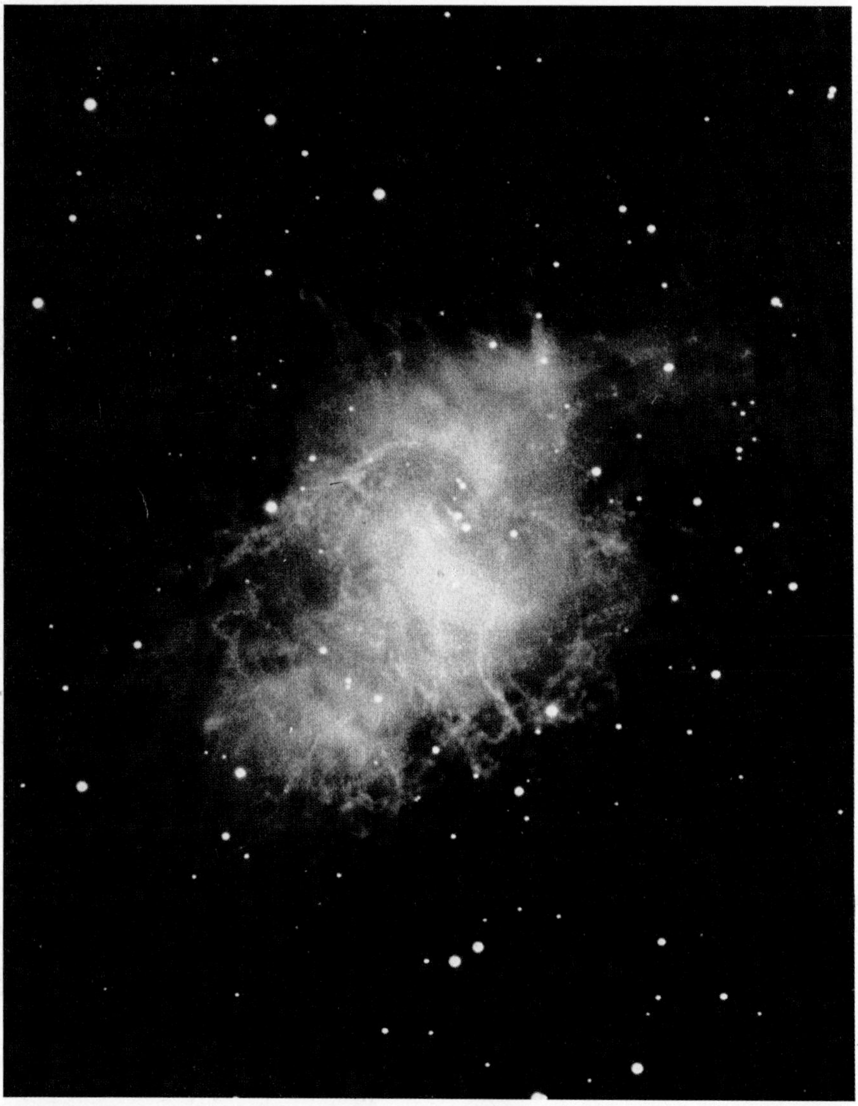

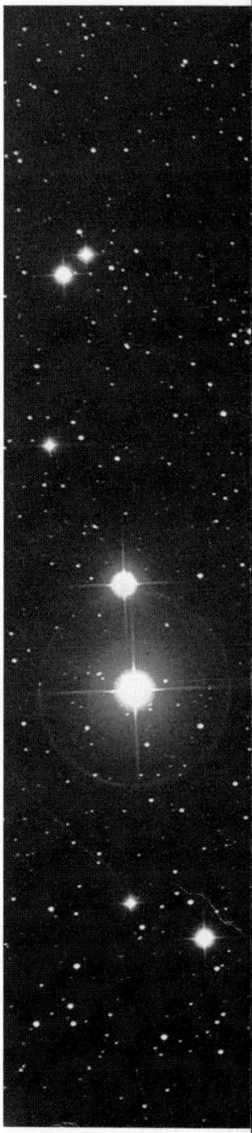

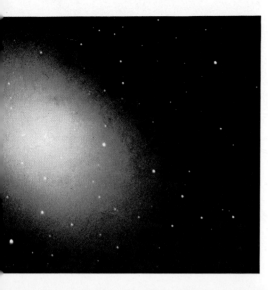

M.33, the Triangulum Spiral *far left* The magnitude of the galaxy is between 6 and 7, so that it is visible in binoculars. It has about one twenty-fifth the mass of our own Galaxy.

Nucleus of Andromeda Spiral, M.31 *left* In most photographs of spirals, the nucleus is over-exposed so as to bring out the structure of the arms; in this view the exposure is correct for the nucleus. Some foreground stars of our Galaxy are seen.

M.1, the Crab Nebula *bottom left* Situated in Taurus, near the third-magnitude star Zeta Tauri. A small telescope will show it as a faint patch. It is the remnant of the 1054 supernova, and is 6,000 light-years away; it is a source of radiations at all wavelengths.

The Pleiades, M.45 *below* This is much the brightest of all open galactic clusters, and is a striking object in the winter sky. The reflection nebulosity shown here is only well studied photographically.

The Northern Sky 4

The North America Nebula, NGC 7000
above Situated in Cygnus. It is 1,000 light-years away, and is apparently associated with the exceptionally luminous supergiant star Deneb; the nickname is unofficial, but the pattern certainly does resemble the shape of the North American continent. Dark areas, due to intervening dust, are also seen.

The Veil or Cirrus Nebula, NGC 6992
above right Also in Cygnus. This is almost certainly a supernova remnant; its distance is 2,500 light-years. The nebula is expanding, and it has been calculated that in 25,000 years' time it will cease to be luminous. The outburst probably occurred 50,000 years ago.

The Ring Nebula, M.57 Lyræ *right* This is the finest example of a planetary nebula; it is easy to find, as it lies midway between the two naked-eye stars Beta and Gamma Lyræ, though in small telescopes it is very faint. It is 1,410 light-years away. Its colour is, of course, too dim to be seen telescopically.

Planetary nebula, NGC 6781 *far right* Situated in Aquarius. It is faint, with a magnitude of below 12, and was not included in Messier's list. It is much less perfectly symmetrical than the Ring Nebula. The stars shown in the photograph are in the foreground; the picture was taken with the 48-in. Schmidt telescope at Palomar, U.S.A.

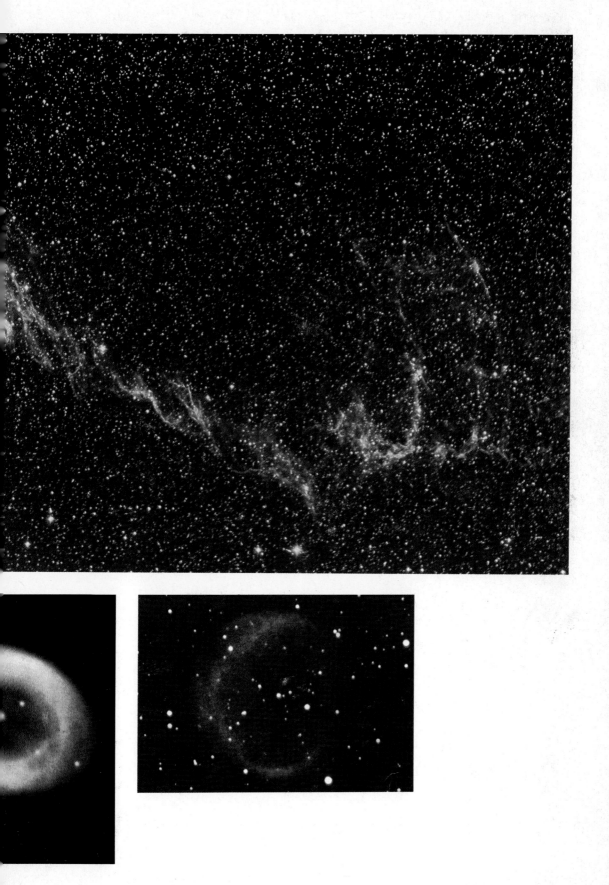

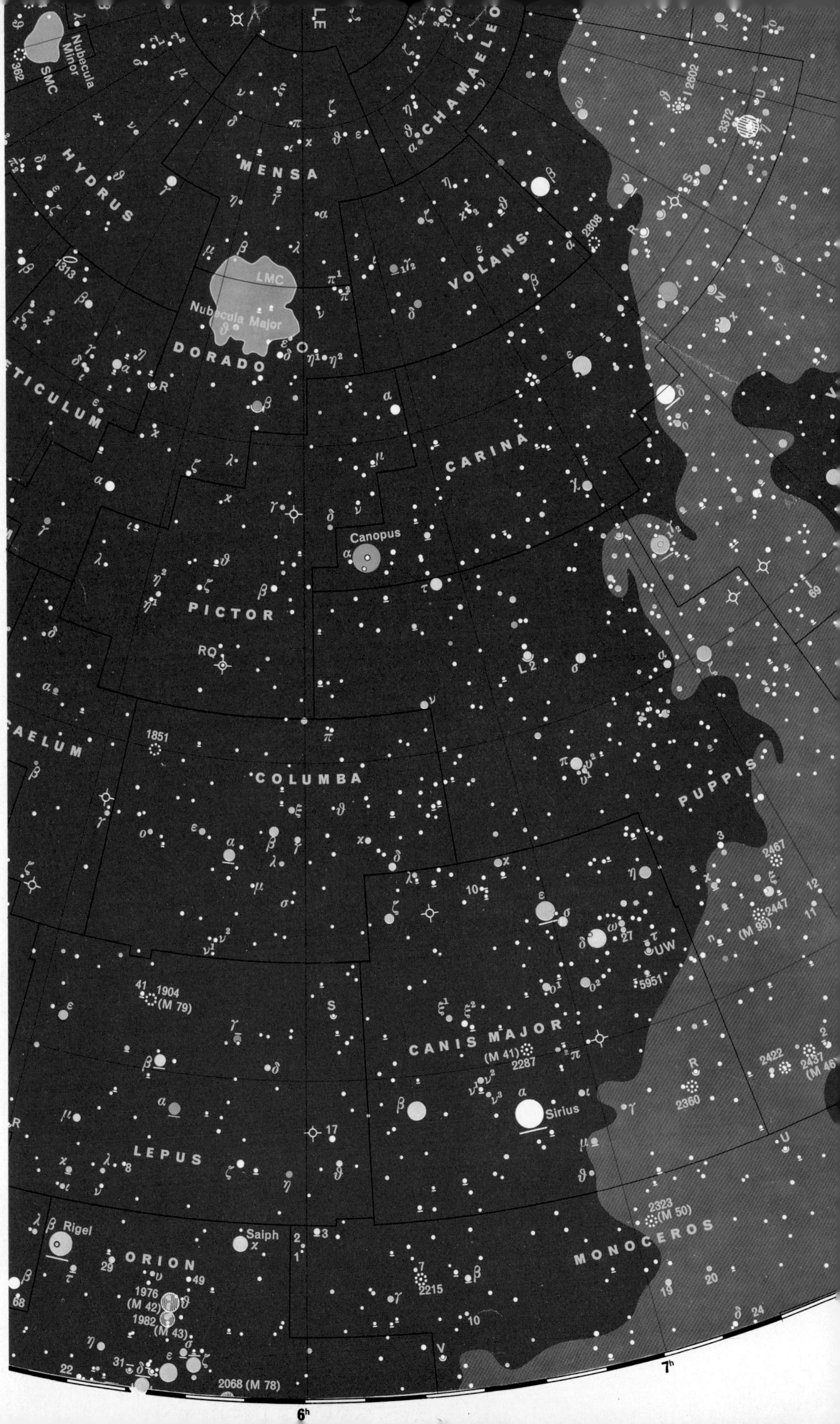

© Hallwag Berne 1973

SMC
Nubecula Minor
362
HYDRUS
1313
MENSA
CHAMAELEON
2602
3372
LMC
Nubecula Major
DORADO
VOLANS
2808
RETICULUM
CARINA
R
CAELUM
Canopus
PICTOR
RQ
69
1851
COLUMBA
PUPPIS
3
2467
2447 (M 93)
12
11
L 2
5951
10
27
UW
CANIS MAJOR
(M 41) 2287
41 1904 (M 79)
S
ξ¹ ξ²
R 2360
2422
2437 (M 46)
Sirius
17
LEPUS
2323 (M 50)
MONOCEROS
R
λ Rigel
Saiph
ORION
29
49
1976 (M 42)
1982 (M 43)
7 2215
13
20
10
2068 (M 78)
V
24

6ʰ   7ʰ

The Southern Sky 1

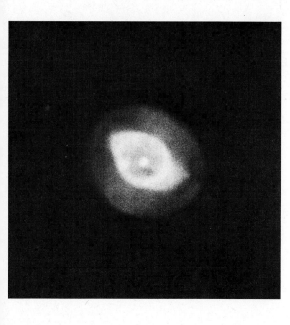

Star-fields in the Milky Way *far left* The streak is the trail of the balloon satellite Echo I, which was a passive radio reflector and was extremely bright. It has long since decayed in the atmosphere. Photographed from the Flagstaff Observatory, Arizona, U.S.A.

Planetary Nebula, NGC 3242 *left* Situated in Hydra. This is a well-marked object, but is of only the 9th magnitude; it is 1,800 light-years away, and its form is clearly different from that of the Ring Nebula in Lyra (page 49). Photographed with the 200-in. reflector at Palomar, U.S.A.

Part of the Great Nebula in Orion, M.42 *below left* This is the most famous of all galactic nebulæ; it lies in the Sword of Orion, close to the Belt, and is easily visible with the naked eye. Photographed with the 200-in. reflector at Palomar, U.S.A.

The Horse's Head Nebula *below* This is part of the nebulosity in Orion, not far from Zeta Orionis in the Belt. The dark nebula certainly does look a little like the shape of a knight's head in chess. The photograph was taken with the 48-in. Schmidt telescope at Palomar, U.S.A.

The Southern Sky 2

The Trifid Nebula, M.20 *above left* Situated in
Sagittarius. Although outstanding photographically,
taken with the Palomar 200-in. telescope, it cannot be
said that the Trifid Nebula is striking when observed
visually. It is of the 9th magnitude, and is a typical
emission nebula; the 'trifid' appearance is due to the
presence of dark matter associated with the nebula. It is
30 light-years away, and is a radio source.

Star-clouds in Sagittarius *above* Two famous
gaseous nebulæ are shown: M.8 (the Lagoon Nebula)
in the centre, and M.20 (the Trifid Nebula) above. In
fact, this picture gives a good impression of what the
area will look like when observed through a telescope of
moderately large aperture and wide field. The Milky Way
is rich in the area. Photographed with the 18-in.
Schmidt telescope at Palomar, U.S.A.

The Omega Nebula, M.17 *far left* Situated in
Sagittarius, and sometimes called the Horseshoe Nebula.
It is of the 7th magnitude, and is easily visible with
binoculars. It is on the borders of Sagittarius and Scutum,
and the best guide-star to it is Gamma Scuti, of
magnitude 4.7. The Omega Nebula is 5,870 light-years
away, and, according to recent estimates, it is more
massive than the Orion Nebula.

M.104, in Virgo *left* Looking at this photograph, one
can easily understand why the galaxy has been
nicknamed the Sombrero Hat! It is an Sb-type spiral at a
distance of 41 million light-years; the dark band is due
to obscuring material lying along the main plane of the
system. It is surrounded by a halo of globular clusters,
similar to the halo which surrounds our own Galaxy.

The Southern Sky 3

The Southern Sky 3

Emission Nebula, M.16 *below* It actually lies in the constellation of Serpens, but is close to the borders of Scutum and Sagittarius; the best guide-star is Gamma Scuti. M.16 is an easy object in binoculars, and lies in a rich part of the Milky Way. Dark nebulosity can also be made out. The nebula is 5,870 light-years from us.

Planetary Nebula, NGC 7293 *below left* Situated in Aquarius. Though this is actually the brightest of all the planetaries, and has an integrated magnitude of $5\frac{1}{2}$— much brighter than that of the Ring Nebula in Lyra—it is not listed by Messier. The nebula is easy to see with a small telescope, but the central star is of below magnitude 13, and is therefore a rather difficult object.

The Lagoon Nebula, M.8 *below* Situated in Sagittarius. This was taken with the Palomar 200-in. reflector, and brings out the colour more clearly than in other views in this book—though let it be repeated that appearances are deceptive, and anyone who expects to see the colours by looking at M.8 through any telescope is doomed to disappointment!

The Southern Sky 4

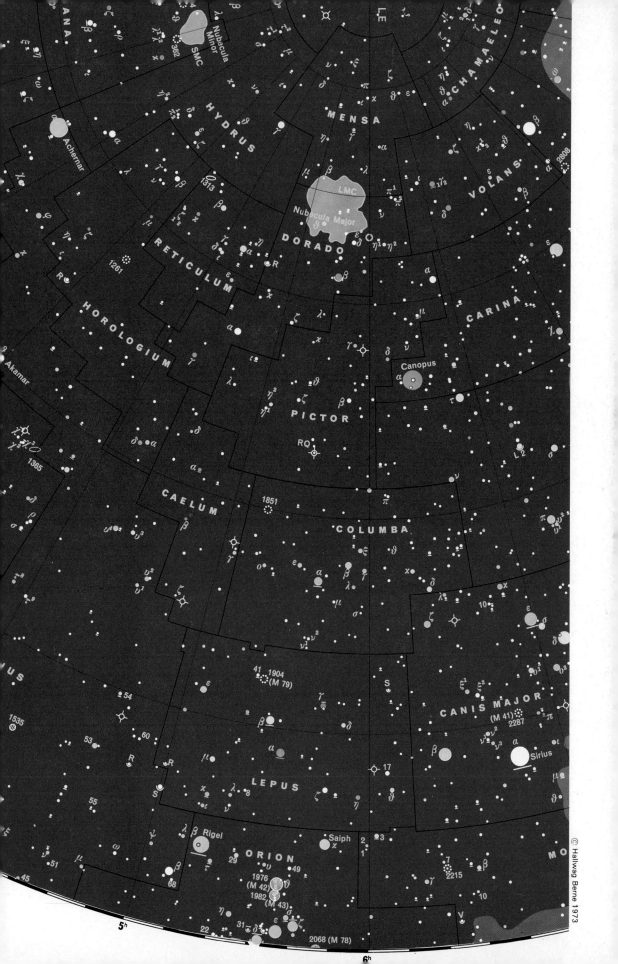

NGC 253, in Sculptor *above* This edge-on spiral is a 9th-magnitude galaxy, but it is placed at an unfavourable angle to us, and the spiral structure is difficult to make out at all.

The Great Nebula in Orion, M.42 *left* The intricate structure is well shown. Photographed with the 200-in. reflector at Palomar, U.S.A.

The Region of Eta Carinæ *upper right* Eta Carinæ once shone as the second brightest star in the sky, but for a century now has been invisible with the naked eye (magnitude 7). Photographed at the Cape Observatory.

A Barred Spiral, NGC 1300 *right* Situated in Eridanus. This is a faint object, with a magnitude of below 11. The bar is extended, with loose arms issuing from both ends of it; the nucleus is small.

30 Doradûs *far right* Part of the great looped nebula in the Large Cloud of Magellan. The nebula is much more extensive than the Orion Nebula—but the Cloud of Magellan is 180,000 light-years away!

OBSERVING THE STARS

It is probably true to say that, so far as amateur astronomy is concerned, the main emphasis is upon the bodies of the Solar System. This has always been natural enough. The Sun, Moon and planets show considerable detail, whereas the stars look like nothing more impressive than twinkling points. Moreover, in former times the average professional astronomer paid little attention to the surfaces of the Moon or planets, and the best maps were of amateur construction.

The present situation is very different. The Space Age is with us; lunar mapping has been completed by means of orbiting probes, and soon the same will be true of Mars. This does not mean that amateur astronomers have no longer a rôle to play. Their work is as important as ever. But because some of their original programmes are now obsolete, more and more are turning their attention to the stars.

In saying this, I do not include the nearest star, the Sun, because solar work involves entirely different techniques. The golden rule is: *Never* look directly at the Sun with any telescope, or even binoculars; to do so is to invite blindness. Also, never use a dark eyepiece-cap for direct viewing. To see sunspots, use the telescope as a projector, but keep your eye well away from the eyepiece.

With the stars, of course, the ideal is to collect as much light as possible—at least so far as most observers are concerned. However, no telescope likely to be in the possession of an amateur will show the nebulæ and galaxies one hundredth as clearly as in the photographs given earlier in this book, and the glorious colours shown in, say, the Palomar photographs of the Orion Nebula and the Andromeda Spiral will remain obstinately invisible. Neither can the amateur undertake theoretical research (unless, of course, he happens to be a mathematician). And yet there are fields of work which have by no means been exhausted.

The most popular of all branches of amateur stellar work relates to variable stars. Some (the Cepheids and RR Lyræ stars) are completely regular, but others are always apt to take us by surprise. Who can tell when R Coronæ will next start to produce one of its spectacular falls to minimum, or when SS Cygni will burst forth from obscurity to the 8th magnitude? Yet it is important to keep a watch on these stars, and this is where the amateur comes in.

For straightforward estimation, no equipment is needed other than an adequate telescope and a set of star-charts. (Some variables are even within binocular range.) The method is to compare the variable with other stars which lie near it, and which do not fluctuate. Suppose that there are two comparison stars in the field, one of magnitude 7.8 and the other of 7.4, and that you judge the variable to be midway between them in brightness; clearly its magnitude must be 7.6. This is admittedly a simplified case, and it often happens that the comparison stars are either inconveniently distant or else awkwardly bright or faint; but with practice it is possible to estimate to an accuracy of a tenth of a magnitude.

Irregular and long-period variable stars are followed consistently by amateurs, and their results are used by professional workers, so that the research is very well worth-while. Moreover, there are some amateurs who occupy themselves with hunting for novæ, and have had spectacular successes. The best equipment here is a pair of powerful, mounted binoculars, since the main requirement is a wide field of view.

There is also useful work to be done with measuring the separations and position angles of double stars, though excellent equipment is needed, and the research is not so easy as it sounds. It is, however, fair to say that some of the reasonably bright pairs have not been measured consistently, and with binaries there are definite shifts in position and separation even over fairly short periods.

Even if you do not have any ambition to undertake scientific research (and this is probably true of most of the readers of this book), it is always fascinating to take a telescope and explore the starlit sky. There is always something new to see, and many of the stellar spectacles are beautiful indeed.

Astronomical telescopes are of various kinds, but they are divided essentially into two types: refractors and reflectors. With the refractor, the light from the distant object is collected by a glass lens, known as an objective or object-glass; with a reflector, the light-collection is done by means of a curved mirror. The aperture of the telescope depends upon the diameter of the object-glass or mirror respectively. Thus a 3-inch refractor has an object-glass 3 inches across, while a 6-inch reflector has a 6-inch mirror. Generally speaking, it is fair to say that inch for inch a lens is more effective than a mirror—though it is also more expensive, and has drawbacks of its own. The smallest telescopes which are really useful astronomically do cost a considerable sum of money if bought new; it is not really sensible to spend much upon any refractor below 3 inches aperture or any reflector below 6 inches.

With the refractor, the light collected by the object-glass is passed down the tube of the telescope and brought to a focus; the image of the body being studied is then magnified by an eyepiece, which is really a special form of magnifying-glass. Note that it is the eyepiece which is responsible for all the magnification; the function of the object-glass is to collect the light—as much light as

is available! The larger the object-glass, the more light can be collected for magnification.

The term 'focal length' is important. This is the distance between the object-glass and the position at which the image is formed. For a 3-inch refractor, the focal length may well be of the order of 36 inches. The 'focal ratio' of the telescope is 36 divided by 3 = 12, often written as f/12.

Every astronomical telescope is equipped with several interchangeable eyepieces. For looking at star-fields one generally needs a wide field of view, with low magnification; for separating close doubles (or, of course, for observing details on planets) it is magnification which is needed. The ideal is to have at least three eyepieces: one low-power, one moderate and one high. It is a general rule that one can obtain a magnification of 50 for every inch of aperture, so that on a 4-inch refractor it should be possible to go up to a magnification of $50 \times 4 = 200$. Remember, however, that you should never try to use too high a magnifying power. It is far better to have a smaller, sharp image than a larger but blurred one.

Unfortunately, it is now difficult to obtain a 3-inch refractor for less than $120, and with spiralling prices this may soon be an underestimate. Lens-making is beyond any average amateur, and second-hand refractors are hard to find—though who knows? You may be lucky!

The Refractor *above* The light is collected by the object-glass and brought to a focus. The image formed is magnified by the eyepiece. In refractors and ordinary reflectors the image is inverted.

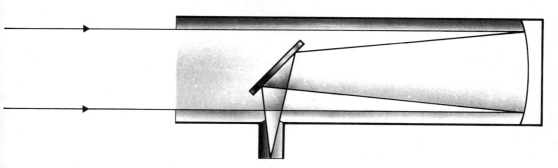

The Newtonian Reflector *above* Light entering the tube is reflected by a curved mirror on to a smaller mirror, the flat. The rays are brought to focus at the side of the tube and magnified by the eyepiece.

Your Own Observatory

Anyone who takes a serious interest in astronomy is bound to ask, 'What sort of telescope should I buy?' This is often where real difficulties begin, because, unfortunately, good astronomical telescopes are not cheap. An instrument which will be useful for proper observation will not cost less than $120 if purchased new; and second-hand telescopes have become depressingly rare in recent years.

All observers will have their own ideas on the minimum useful apertures, and all I can do is to give my own views, realizing that some people will challenge them. I do not regard it as sensible to spend much money on a refractor below 3-in. aperture, or a reflector below 6-in. Smaller telescopes can give pretty views of star-fields, but for an outlay of, say, $35 to $50 I would vastly prefer a pair of good binoculars. These will have most of the advantages of a small telescope, with few of the drawbacks. They will not show the rings of Saturn or the spiral form of the Whirlpool Galaxy, but they will give splendid views of star-fields, clusters and coloured stars, as well as showing objects such as the craters of the Moon and the four bright satellites of Jupiter. A good all-purpose pair of binoculars is the 7×50 variety (magnification 7, aperture of each object-glass, 50 millimetres).

If funds permit, then obviously a telescope is highly desirable; but unless you are an expert in optics, have it checked before purchasing! Also, ensure that the mounting is firm. If the telescope stand is like a jelly, the instrument will quiver alarmingly, and will be virtually useless. On the whole, a 6-in. reflector is probably ideal for the serious newcomer to astronomy. It may be mounted on a straightforward stand, so that it can be swung to any part of the sky and is free to move; this is the altazimuth mount, and is convenient in some ways, although it cannot be used for photography and cannot be clock-driven. For most purposes it is better to have an equatorial mount, in which the telescope is set upon a polar axis which is parallel to the axis of the Earth. This means that as a star goes across the sky, the telescope can be driven round so as to follow it, and only a motion in an east–west direction will be needed; the up-or-down movement, according to

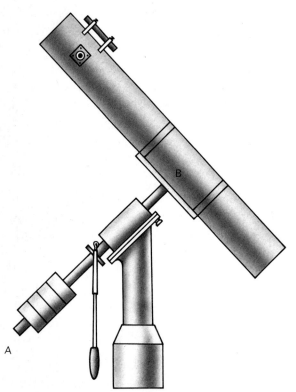

Equatorial Mounting for Newtonian Reflector *above* The polar axis AB points to the celestial pole; the telescope is set on this axis. At A there is a counterweight to balance the mass of the telescope. The handle hanging down is for slow motion in azimuth (east/west). On this mount, a telescope can be driven by a motor.

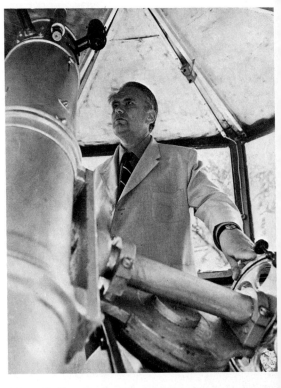

8½-in. Reflector *above* The author inside the dome of his 8½-in. reflector at Selsey. This is on a German-type mount; it has a polar axis and a counterweight. The drive is electrical; there are two finder telescopes, and the tube can be fully rotated in its cradle, thus avoiding the danger of the eyepiece getting into awkward positions

Telescope Housing *above* The run-off shed covering the author's 12½-in. reflector at Selsey. The shed is built in two halves, which run back along the rails in opposite directions when the telescope is to be used. This is probably better than a single shed with a door, because the door must be either hinged or removable; a hinged door is liable to flap, and a removable door can easily act as a powerful sail.

whether the star is rising or setting, will look after itself.

Small telescopes can be moved around, but in general it may be said that any refractor above 4-in. aperture or any Newtonian reflector above 6-in. aperture is non-portable. Therefore it needs a permanent housing. One easy solution is the run-off shed, which is cheap and convenient; neither is it unsightly. A revolving dome is naturally better, but is less easy to make.

It is seldom possible to command a full view of the sky. The amateur astronomer has to contend with hazards such as trees and street lights, and according to Spode's Law (if things *can* be awkward, they *are*), trees always lie in the most inconvenient possible positions. Never attempt to set up an observatory on the roof of a house; the heated air rising from the house will ruin the definition. It is better to select a site as far away as possible from one's house, though of course it is essential to have as clear a view of the sky as can be managed.

The maintenance of the equipment is always something to be borne in mind. If carefully handled, a refractor will not need renovating for years on end; but the mirrors of a reflector have to be periodically re-coated with silver, aluminium or some such reflecting substance, and no telescope can be expected to give of its best unless it is well looked after. Remember never to rub a mirror or a lens. Optical equipment is always delicate.

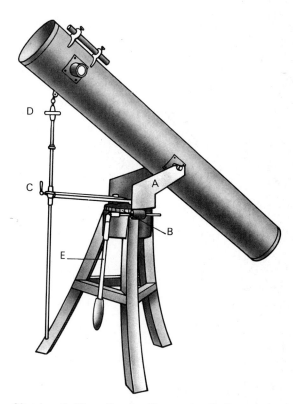

Altazimuth Mounting for Newtonian Reflector *above* The telescope is set in a fork (A) and the fork rotates (B); slow motions are at C for the up-or-down motion, achieved by rotating the wheel D, and the slow motion in azimuth is controlled by the handle E. No drive can be fitted to an ordinary altazimuth mount.

THE CONSTELLATION CHARTS

The seasonal charts show which stars are to be seen at any particular moment. The maps which follow them are intended to act as a guide for observers equipped with binoculars or small telescopes. Proper names of stars are not used except for the stars of the first magnitude and a few other exceptional cases (such as Mizar in the Great Bear). The Greek letters are listed here:

α Alpha	ι Iota	ρ Rho
β Beta	κ Kappa	σ Sigma
γ Gamma	λ Lambda	τ Tau
δ Delta	μ Mu	υ Upsilon
ε Epsilon	ν Nu	φ Phi
ζ Zeta	ξ Xi	χ Chi
η Eta	ο Omicron	ψ Psi
θ Theta	π Pi	ω Omega

I have found that the best way to learn the star-patterns is to select a very few of the major groups and use them as guides to the rest. Orion,

Orion and its Surroundings *below* Orion, the Hunter, a guide to other stars and constellations in its area.
α (Betelgeux) and β (Rigel) are of the 1st magnitude; γ (Bellatrix), δ (Mintaka), ε (Alnilam), ζ (Alnitak) and κ (Saiph) are around the 2nd.

for instance, is unmistakable; it has two brilliant 1st-magnitude stars, Betelgeux and Rigel, and the pattern is very distinctive. There are three 2nd-magnitude stars making up the Hunter's Belt; δ (Mintaka), ε (Alnilam) and ζ (Alnitak). In one direction the Belt stars point to Sirius, in Canis Major, the most brilliant star in the sky; in the opposite direction they show the way to Aldebaran, the red Eye of the Bull. Also to be found from Orion are various others stars, such as Procyon, Capella, Castor and Pollux.

Orion is cut through by the celestial equator, which passes very near Mintaka in the Belt. It is therefore visible from every inhabited country in the world, but it cannot always be seen. In northern summer or southern-hemisphere winter (around June) it is too near the Sun in the sky, and is above the horizon only during daylight, so that it is out of view.

The Great Bear, or Ursa Major, is equally distinctive, though it is not so bright, and contains no star of the 1st magnitude. It lies in the far north, and the two pointers, β (Merak) and α (Dubhe) indicate the Pole Star, or Polaris, in Ursa Minor. On the far side of Polaris lies the

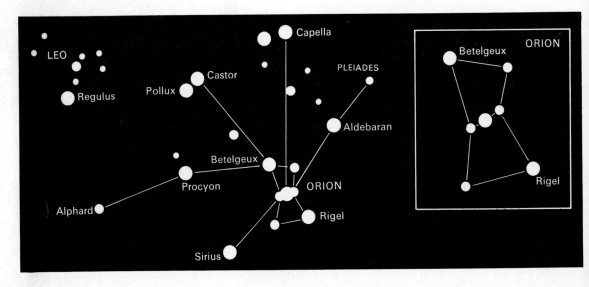

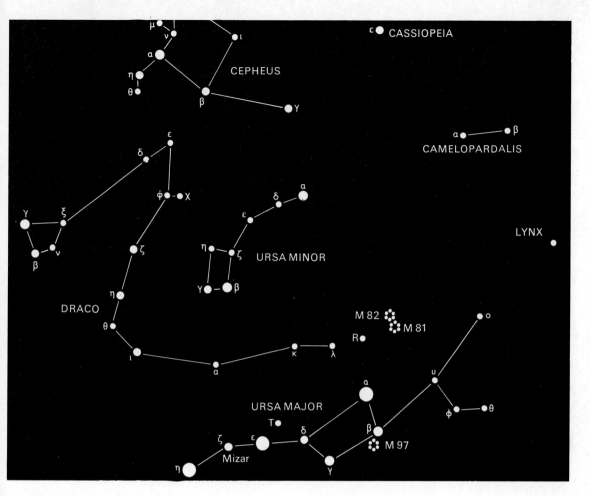

constellation of Cepheus; and so on. From Great Britain, Ursa Major never sets, but from the southernmost countries, such as New Zealand, it can never be seen at all.

The stars in the far south are more brilliant than those of the far north—but there is no bright south polar star. Indeed, the south pole lies in a particularly barren region. The best way to locate it is to use the longer axis of the kite-shaped Southern Cross. If sufficiently prolonged across the sky, the line passing through the two Cross stars will eventually reach the brilliant Achernar, in Eridanus (the River); the pole is then about midway between Achernar and the Cross.

The method I adopted, when setting out to learn the stars, was to begin with the Great Bear and Orion, and then identify at least one new constellation per night. Since there are only 88 constellations all told, and by no means all of these can be seen from England, the whole procedure did not take nearly so long as might be expected; and I recommend it to others.

You will sometimes find a brilliant object which is not on your maps. This will certainly be a planet, and planets cannot be marked on permanent charts, since they wander about.

The North Polar Area *above* Ursa Major, the Great Bear. It is a splendid guide to other stars; β and α indicate Polaris, and the curve of ε, ζ and η will, if prolonged, come first to Arcturus and then to Spica.

The South Polar Area *below* The main constellation is Crux Australis, the Southern Cross; the two brilliant stars α and β Centauri point to it. Canopus, also shown here, is inferior only to Sirius.

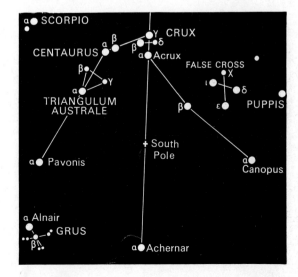

Seasonal Charts: North 1

Observer's view *right* looking north *far right* looking south. The latitude marks at the bottom of the charts indicate the level of the horizon for an observer at the given latitude. Dates and times refer to both charts.

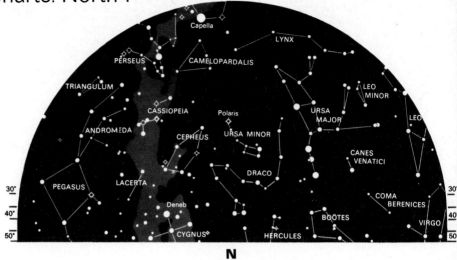

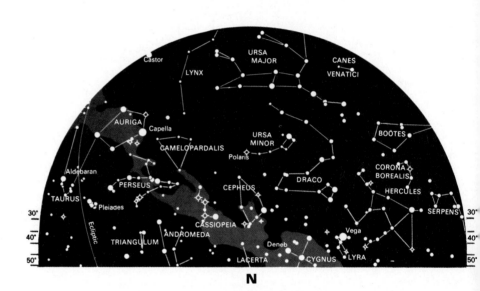

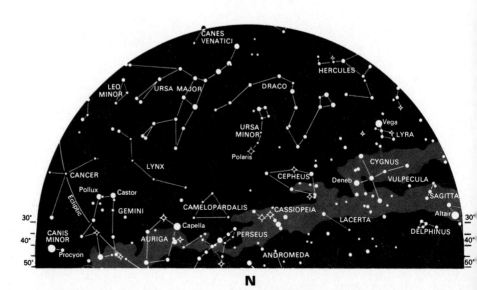

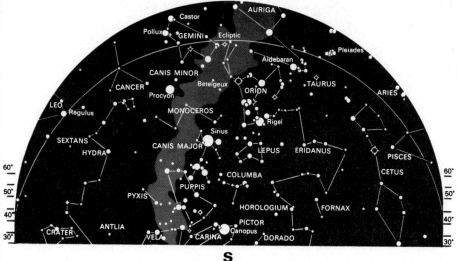

Morning
October 1 at 5.30
October 15 at 4.30
October 30 at 3.30

Evening
January 1 at 11.30
January 15 at 10.30
January 30 at 9.30

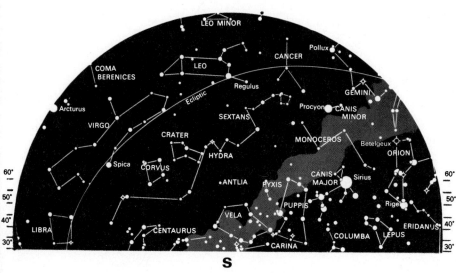

Morning
November 15 at 6.30
December 1 at 5.30
December 15 at 4.30

Evening
March 1 at 11.30
March 15 at 10.30
March 30 at 9.30

Morning
January 15 at 6.30
February 1 at 5.30
February 14 at 4.30

Evening
May 1 at 11.30
May 15 at 10.30
May 30 at 9.30

Seasonal Charts: North 2

Observer's view *right* looking north *far right* looking south. The latitude marks at the bottom of the charts indicate the level of the horizon for an observer at the given latitude. Dates and times refer to both charts.

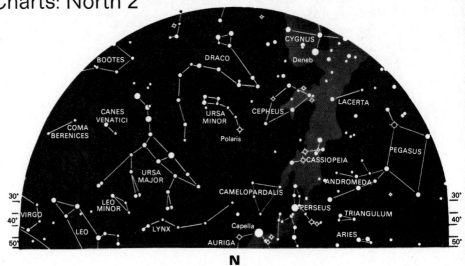

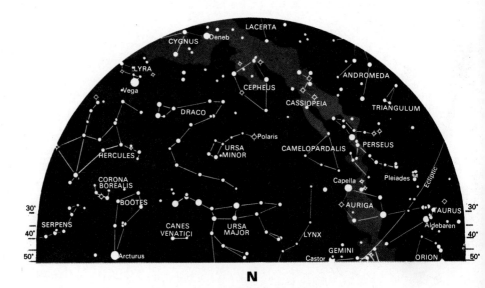

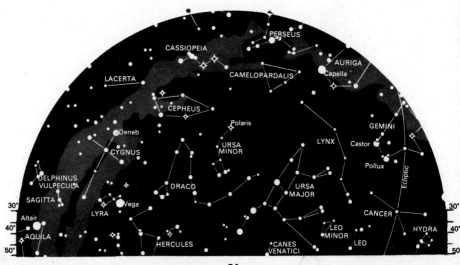

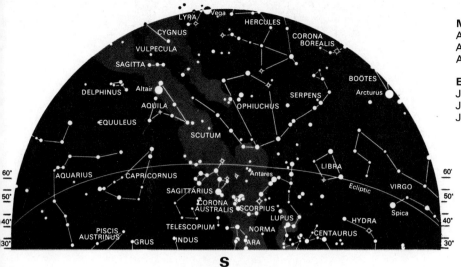

Morning
April 1 at 5.30
April 15 at 4.30
April 30 at 3.30

Evening
July 1 at 11.30
July 15 at 10.30
July 30 at 9.30

Morning
June 15 at 4.30
June 30 at 3.30
July 15 at 2.30

Evening
September 1 at 11.30
September 15 at 10.30
September 30 at 9.30

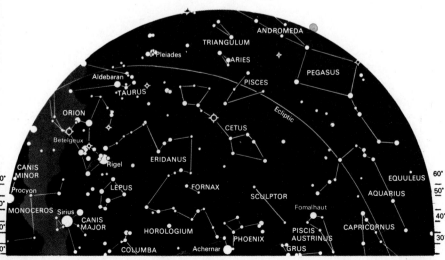

Morning
August 15 at 4.30
August 30 at 3.30
September 15 at 2.30

Evening
November 1 at 11.30
November 15 at 10.30
November 30 at 9.30

Seasonal Charts: South 1

Observer's view *right* looking north *far right* looking south. The latitude marks at the bottom of the charts indicate the level of the horizon for an observer at the given latitude. Dates and times refer to both charts.

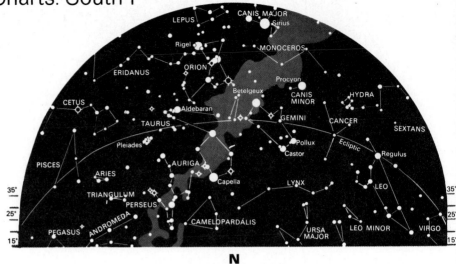

N

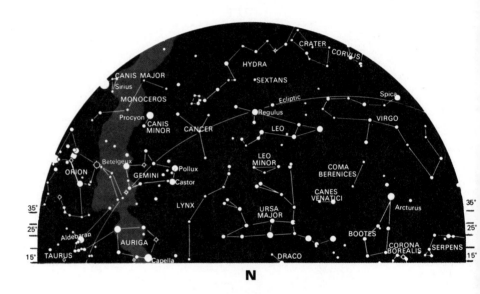

N

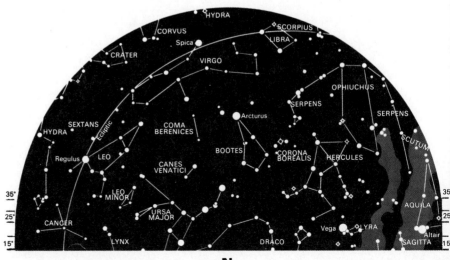

N

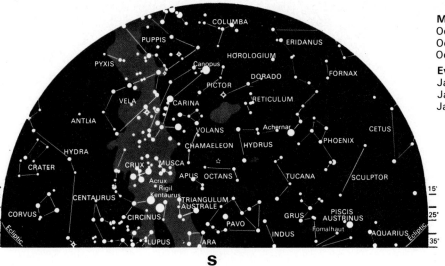

Morning
October 1 at 5.30
October 15 at 4.30
October 30 at 3.30

Evening
January 1 at 11.30
January 15 at 10.30
January 30 at 9.30

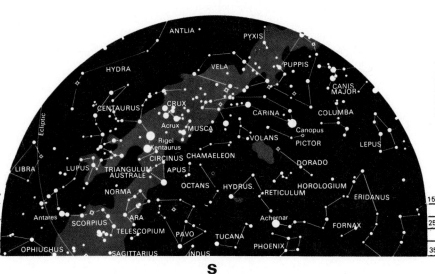

Morning
December 15 at 4.30
December 30 at 3.30
January 15 at 2.30

Evening
March 1 at 11.30
March 15 at 10.30
March 30 at 9.30

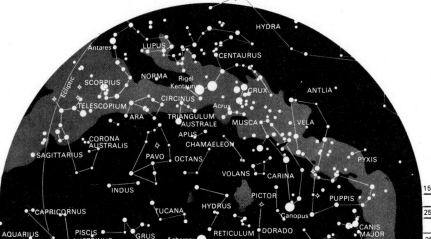

Morning
February 14 at 4.30
February 28 at 3.30
March 15 at 2.30

Evening
May 1 at 11.30
May 15 at 10.30
May 30 at 9.30

77

Seasonal Charts: South 2

Observer's view *right* looking north *far right* looking south. The latitude marks at the bottom of the charts indicate the level of the horizon for an observer at the given latitude. Dates and times refer to both charts.

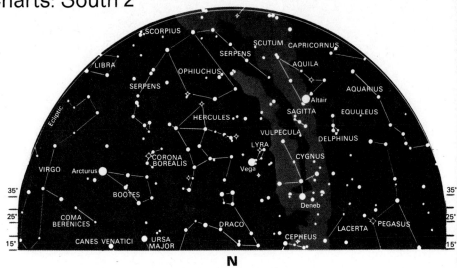

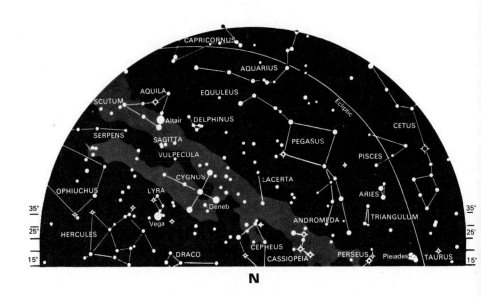

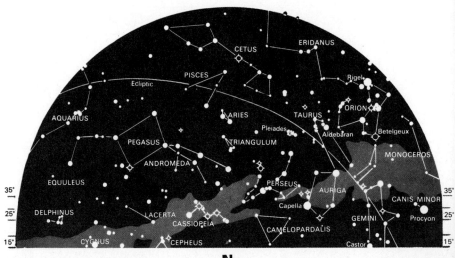

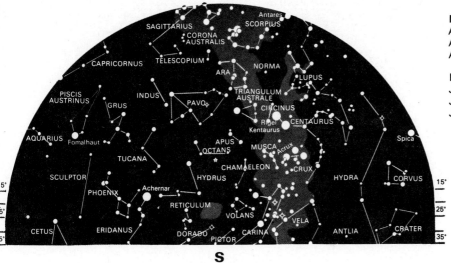

Morning
April 1 at 5.30
April 15 at 4.30
April 30 at 3.30

Evening
July 1 at 11.30
July 15 at 10.30
July 30 at 9.30

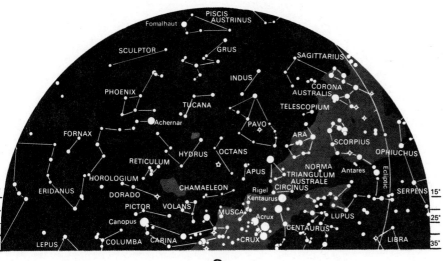

Morning
May 15 at 6.30
June 1 at 5.30
June 15 at 4.30

Evening
September 1 at 11.30
September 15 at 10.30
September 30 at 9.30

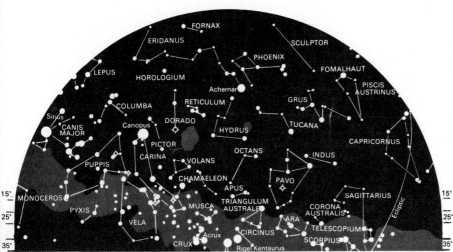

Morning
July 15 at 6.30
August 1 at 5.30
August 15 at 4.30

Evening
November 1 at 11.30
November 15 at 10.30
November 30 at 9.30

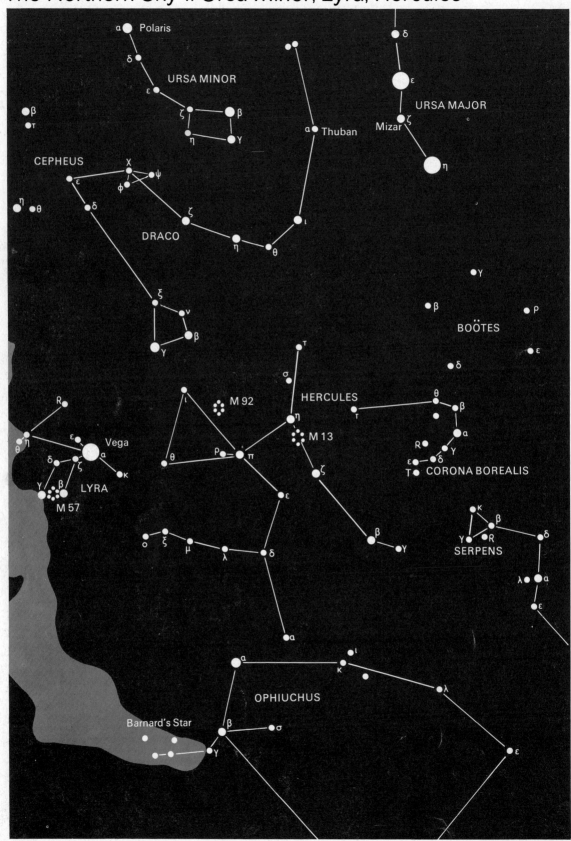

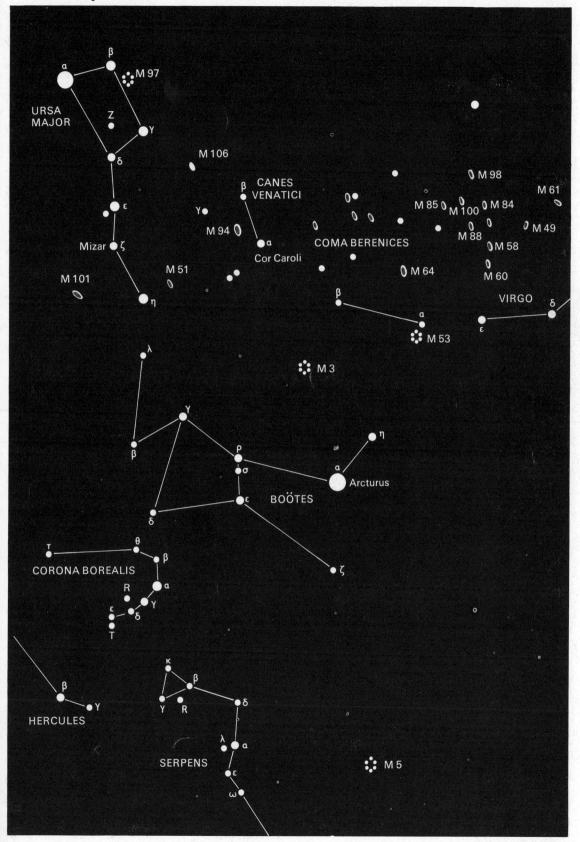

The Northern Sky 1: Notes

These charts show some of the most important constellations of the far northern sky, notably Ursa Major. Two 1st-magnitude stars are included in the charts: Arcturus in Boötes, and Vega in Lyra.

Ursa Minor. The Little Bear. This is the north polar constellation, and contains Polaris, which is within one degree of the pole itself. Both it and β (Kocab) are of magnitude 2.0. The next brightest star in Ursa Minor is γ, which is just below the 3rd magnitude.

Ursa Minor is easy to identify because of its position, but it is not a conspicuous group, and under moonlight or misty conditions only its three brightest stars are likely to be visible with the naked eye. On a clear night, however, the pattern is obviously similar to that of the Plough, though much fainter and distorted. Polaris has a 9th-magnitude companion at 18″.3, easy to see with a modest telescope, and Kocab is a fine orange star of spectral type K.

Ursa Major. The Great Bear. It is a large constellation; the famous seven-star pattern of the Plough or Big Dipper is merely a part of it. There are six stars above the 3rd magnitude; ε (Alioth) (1.8), α (Dubhe) (1.8), η (Alkaid) (1.9), ζ (Mizar) (2.1), β (Merak) (2.4) and γ (Phad) (2.4). The seventh star of the Plough pattern, δ (Megrez) is of magnitude 3.3.

The most interesting of the Plough stars is Mizar. Close to it lies 80 Ursæ Majoris, or Alcor, which is easily visible with the naked eye on a clear night. With even a small telescope, Mizar itself is seen to be double; one component is decidedly brighter than the other, and the separation between them is 14.5 seconds of arc. Between the bright pair and Alcor is another star, which is not connected with any of the Mizar group and merely happens to lie in about the same direction.

There are various galaxies in Ursa Major—notably the spiral M.101—but all are too faint to be seen well with small telescopes. Z, in the 'bowl', is a semi-regular variable star, visible with binoculars.

Canes Venatici. The Hunting Dogs. Circumpolar in Britain, with one bright star, α (Cor Caroli), magnitude 2.9. It is a wide optical double; magnitudes 3 and 5.6, distance 20″. There are various clusters and nebulæ; M.3 is a bright globular, and M.94 a spiral with tightly-wound arms and a condensed nucleus. Also in

Canes Venatici, though not far from Alkaid in Ursa Major, is the Whirlpool Galaxy, M.51. It is of magnitude 8, though large apertures are needed to show the characteristic spiral structure of the galaxy.

Coma Berenices. Berenice's Hair. At first glance this area looks like a wide, scattered cluster. There are no bright stars, but there are many faint galaxies, and the whole area is so rich that it is well worth scanning with binoculars. Adjoining it is Virgo, most of which lies in the southern hemisphere (see pages 100 and 102); ε Virginis (magnitude 2.9) is shown on page 81; nearby there are an exceptional number of galaxies.

Draco. The Dragon. This is a long, winding constellation, extending from near Vega over to the area between the pointers in Ursa Major and Polaris. There are three stars above the 3rd magnitude: γ (2.2), η (2.7) and β (2.8). The much fainter Thuban, which is lettered α in the constellation, is only of magnitude 3.6, but it used to be important, since it was the pole star in ancient times.

Draco does not contain many interesting objects, but it is worth looking at ν, in the Dragon's Head. This is made up of two components, each of magnitude 4.3, and 62″ apart, so that any optical power will separate them, and keen-sighted people can split the pair with the naked eye.

Lyra. The Harp or Lyre. The constellation is led by Vega, which is of magnitude 0.0 and is the brightest star in the northern hemisphere apart from Arcturus (though Arcturus, Vega and Capella are practically equal). Vega is distinguished by its obviously bluish colour. During summer evenings it is very high up when viewed from Britain, and it never sets over any part of the British Isles, though from some latitudes it can almost graze the horizon.

Lyra contains no other star above the 3rd magnitude, but there is one very important variable. This is β, which has a range from 3.4 to 4.4 and a period of 12.9 days. It is an eclipsing binary; the components cannot be seen separately, and must be almost in contact. The star is always in variation, with alternate deep and shallow minima. Its fluctuations may be followed with the naked eye; the adjacent star γ (magnitude 3.2) makes a suitable comparison.

Another variable is R, which ranges from magnitude 4 to 5 in a very rough period of seven weeks. It is classed as semi-regular, and, like most of its kind, is a red giant. It is not particularly easy to estimate, as there are no good comparison stars near it; I use η and θ (each magnitude 4.5).

Close to Vega is ε, which is a naked-eye double. The magnitudes are 4.5 and 4.7 respectively, and the separation is 208″. A 3-inch telescope will show that each component is again double; the separations are 2″.8 and 2″.2 respectively. We have here a true multiple system. Several unconnected stars are in the same low-power field. Another double, though not separable without a telescope, is ζ: magnitudes 4.3 and 5.9, separation 44″.

Finally, note M.57, the Ring Nebula, a fine planetary, shown on page 48. It is not bright, but is easy to find, as it lies midway between β and γ.

Hercules. The only two stars above the 3rd magnitude are β and ζ, each 2.8. The pattern is not distinctive, and Hercules is not one of the easier constellations to identify.

The most interesting objects are the two globular clusters, M.13 and M.92, and the red variable α (Rasalgethi). M.13 is just visible with the naked eye under good conditions, and is a fine sight in a moderate telescope. M.92, between ι and η, is slightly smaller and more condensed; it is only just below naked-eye visibility, and is not much inferior to the more famous M.13.

Rasalgethi is variable between magnitudes 3 and 4; there is no definite period. The best comparison star is κ Ophiuchi (3.4). Rasalgethi is a huge red giant. It has a companion of magnitude 5.4, at 4″.6, which is distinctly greenish; the hue is exaggerated by contrast with the red primary.

Corona Borealis. The Northern Crown. There is a prominent semicircle of stars, headed by α (Alphekka) which is of magnitude 2.2. The irregular variable R Coronæ, which lies in the 'bowl' of the Crown, is on the fringe of naked-eye visibility, and easy with any optical aid; but at unpredictable intervals it fades, sinking to well below magnitude 12 before recovering. It is the typical star of its class, and has been closely studied. Also in the bowl is a star of magnitude 6.6; if you use binoculars and find that only one of the two stars is visible, you may be sure that R Coronæ is going through a minimum. On the other hand, it may stay near maximum for years at a time, showing little variation.

Of equal interest is T Coronæ, sometimes called the Blaze Star. Generally it is of about the 10th magnitude, so that it is visible with a small telescope or even in powerful binoculars, but twice— in 1866 and again in 1946—it has risen abruptly to the 2nd magnitude, remaining bright for only a

short while before fading back to its normal obscurity. It seems to form a link between irregular variable stars and novæ, and is classed as a 'recurrent nova'. It is not unique; a few other recurrent novæ are known, but T Coronæ is the most celebrated of them. If it bursts forth only once in every eighty years we cannot expect it to do so again before the end of our present century, but one never knows, and it is well worth watching.

Boötes. The Herdsman. Boötes is dominated by Arcturus, which is of magnitude −0.1 and surpassed only by Sirius and Canopus. To find it, follow round the tail of the Great Bear; Arcturus is so brilliant that it can hardly be mis-identified, particularly in view of its lovely light orange colour. The only other stars in Boötes above the 3rd magnitude are ε (2.4) and η (2.7), and there is no really obvious pattern.

ε, sometimes still known by its old proper name of Izar, is double; the primary is yellowish and the 5th magnitude companion bluish. As the separation is 3″, it is not a difficult object. δ is also double; the magnitudes are 3.5 and 7.7, and the distance is 105″, so that it is a very easy pair.

Ophiuchus. The Serpent-bearer. There is one bright star, α (Rasalhague) of magnitude 2.1, which lies close to Rasalgethi; it is not hard to locate, as it is rather isolated. Barnard's Star, shown on the chart, is of magnitude $9\frac{1}{2}$, and is the nearest star apart from members of the α Centauri group; it is six light-years from us, and nicknamed the Runaway Star because of its large proper motion. It is not easy to identify.

The celestial equator runs through Ophiuchus, so that only part of the constellation is shown on this chart. Further south in the sky part of Ophiuchus intrudes into the Zodiac, so that planets may be found in it—though Ophiuchus is not ranked as a Zodiacal constellation.

Serpens. The Serpent, with which Ophiuchus is apparently struggling; the section shown here is Caput (the Head). The brightest star is α, magnitude 2.6. The actual head is marked by a triangle of rather inconspicuous stars; it also includes a long-period variable, R Serpentis, which can be just visible with the naked eye at maximum but becomes too faint at minimum to be seen with small telescopes. The period is 357 days, and during the early 1970s it was reaching maximum when too near the Sun to be observed.

Some way from α Serpentis lies a globular cluster, M.5. This is easily visible with binoculars, and is bright and condensed; with the exception of M.13 Herculis, it is the finest globular visible from Britain. It is 27,000 light-years from us, and is very rich.

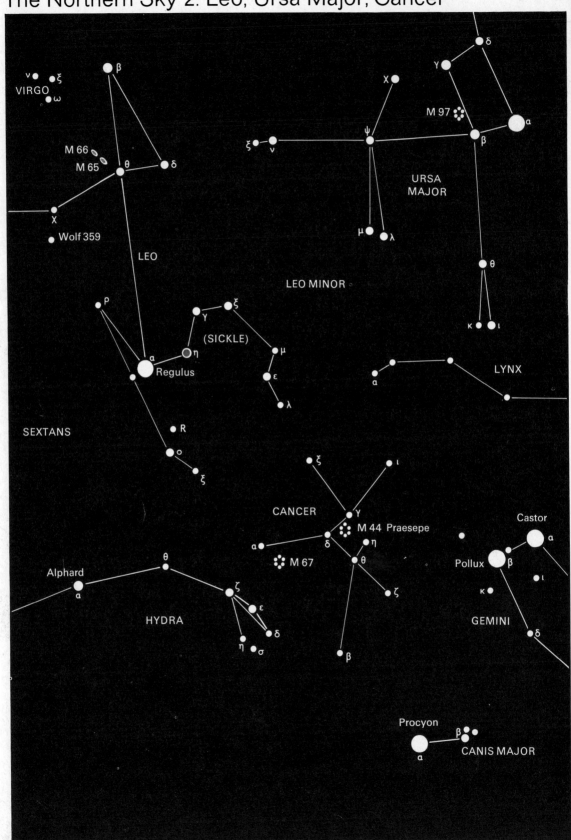

Ursa Major, Gemini, Auriga, Orion

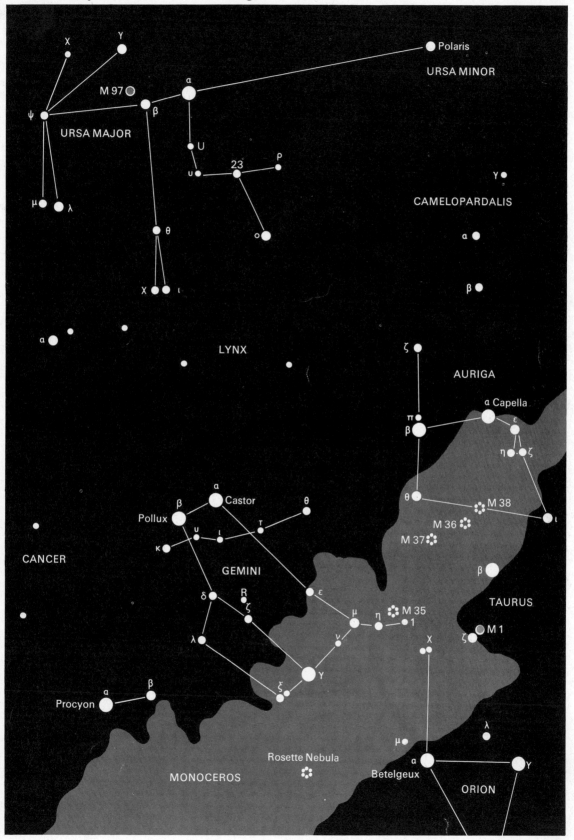

The Northern Sky 2: Notes

These charts include some extremely rich regions crossed by the Milky Way; Auriga and Gemini are splendid constellations, and we also have the northern part of Orion. On the other hand the charts also show Camelopardalis and Lynx, which are among the darkest, most barren areas in the entire sky.

The 1st-magnitude stars shown are Capella in Auriga, Betelgeux in Orion, Procyon in Canis Minor, Pollux in Gemini and Regulus in Leo. Castor, also in Gemini is only slightly below the 1st magnitude.

Leo. The Lion. A large and prominent constellation; over northern countries such as Britain it is best seen during spring evenings. The leader, Regulus (α), is of the first magnitude. Extending from it is a curved line of stars marking what is unofficially called the Sickle; and some way away there is a well-marked triangle. Apart from Regulus, there are three stars above the 3rd magnitude: γ (2.0), β (2.1) and δ (2.6).

β, or Denebola, was ranked of the 1st magnitude by Ptolemy in the second century A.D., but is now far inferior to Regulus; it has been suspected of slight variability in modern times, though the evidence is very slender. γ is a fine binary, with a period of 407 years; the separation is over 4″, and the components are of magnitudes 2 and 3.8, so that this is a very easy object. Not far from Regulus is R Leonis, a typical Mira-type variable, with a range from magnitude 5 to 10.5 and a period of 312 days. It is a naked-eye object when at maximum (or generally so; as with all stars of its kind, the maxima are not equally bright) and with good binoculars all its fluctuations can be followed.

Wolf 259 is shown on the map, but is not easy to find, as its apparent magnitude is below 13. It is an exceptionally feeble red dwarf, with a luminosity of 0.00002 that of the Sun; it is 8 light-years from us.

Leo Minor. The Little Lion. A very small, dim and unremarkable constellation between Leo and Ursa Major. It hardly seems to merit a separate name.

Ursa Major. Part of the Great Bear is shown, including the two pointers, α (Dubhe) and β (Merak). Ursa Major extends out towards Gemini; there are several stars between magnitudes 3 and 4, but nothing of special note apart from M.97, the so-called Owl Nebula near Merak. This is a planetary, but is different from the Ring Nebula in

Lyra, as there are two stars in it—giving it the aspect of an owl's face. It is 10,000 light-years from us. It was discovered as long ago as 1781 (by the French astronomer Méchain), but is only of the 12th magnitude, so is hard to see with most amateur-owned telescopes.

Camelopardalis. The Giraffe. This is a large but extremely faint constellation. There are no stars above the 4th magnitude.

Sextans. The Sextant. This adjoins Hydra. It contains no bright stars, and is entirely unremarkable.

Lynx. The Lynx. This group is devoid of bright stars or notable objects.

Auriga. The Charioteer or Wagoner. Here we come to one of the really splendid constellations of the northern hemisphere. The brightest stars are α (Capella) (0.0); β (1.9), θ and ι (2.6). Capella is of course dominant, and is near the zenith or overhead point during winter evenings in Great Britain and the northern United States. A double check is provided by the triangle of three fainter stars close beside it, known as the Haedi or Kids—η, ε and ζ.

Capella is a glorious yellow, indicating that its surface temperature is much the same as that of the Sun; it too is of spectral type G. However, it is a giant, with a luminosity 150 times that of the Sun. It is a very close binary; the components are hardly separable with any telescope.

Auriga is fairly distinctive in shape, as Capella, β, θ and ι make a quadrilateral. Slightly further south is the bright star Alnath, or β Tauri. Originally Alnath was included in Auriga; the original reason for its transfer to Taurus seems unknown.

Two of the Kids, ζ and ε, are eclipsing binaries of unusual type, with supergiant primaries and very long periods (972 days and $27\frac{1}{2}$ years respectively); the secondary component in ε may even be a collapsar, though on this point authorities are not in agreement.

M.36, M.37 and M.38 are bright galactic clusters, easily visible in binoculars.

Hydra. The Watersnake. Hydra has the distinction of being the largest constellation in the whole sky, but it is remarkably barren, and contains only one bright star. This is α or Alphard, the Solitary One, which is of magnitude 2.0 and is clearly reddish; Castor and Pollux point to it.

The Watersnake's head is also shown, but the brightest star in it, ζ, is below the 3rd magnitude.

Cancer. The Crab. Like Taurus, Gemini and Leo, this is a Zodiacal constellation; but it is relatively obscure, and contains no star brighter than magnitude 3.8. ζ is notable as being a binary with a period of 60 years; the components are of magnitudes 5 and 5.7, and the separation is about 1″. There is a third component, of the 6th magnitude, at a distance of almost 6″.

Cancer is interesting mainly because of its two bright clusters, M.44 and M.67. M.44 is known as Præsepe, or the Beehive, and is the finest of all open clusters visible from Europe apart from the Pleiades and the Hyades. It is easily visible with the naked eye on a moonless night, and is excellently seen with binoculars. Because many of its leading stars are yellow or orange, and there is no nebulosity, it is believed that the cluster is much older than the Pleiades. The late Walter Baade, an American astronomer who spent a lifetime studying stellar evolution, estimated its age as 400 million years. Its distance from us is over 500 light-years.

M.67 is clearly visible with binoculars. It lies near α Cancri, which is a 4th-magnitude star, and it is thought to be one of the very oldest of the galactic clusters; most estimates give it an age of between 4,000 and 5,000 million years.

The best way to find Cancer is to look between Regulus in Leo and the Twins, Castor and Pollux. The Crab has a slight resemblance to a very dim and ghostly Orion; Præsepe is flanked to either side by two 4th-magnitude stars, δ and γ, known as the Aselli, or Asses—a reference to the old nickname for Præsepe, which was the Manger.

Gemini. The Twins. One of the most splendid of all the northern constellations. Of its two leaders, β (Pollux) is of magnitude 1.2 and α (Castor) of magnitude 1.6; Pollux is therefore appreciably the brighter, though according to ancient astronomers it used to be the fainter. We cannot say with any confidence that a change has occurred; it is unwise to rely too much on the old records. If there has been any alteration, the change is more likely to have been in Pollux than in Castor. The Twins also differ in colour; Pollux is an orange star of type K, while Castor is white. As we have noted earlier, Castor is a complex multiple-star system.

The two main components may be separated with a fairly small telescope, though the separation is now below 2″; at their widest, in 1880, the separation distance was over 6″. The period is 380 years.

Of the other leading stars in Gemini, γ (Alhena) is of magnitude 1.9; μ and ε are 3.0. δ is double;

the primary is of magnitude 3.5 and the companion 8.2. The separation is 6″.7, and the pair is a light test for a 2-in. refractor.

There are several notable variables in Gemini. ζ is a typical Cepheid, fluctuating between magnitudes 3.7 and 4.3 in a period of 10.2 days; η is a semi-regular variable, with a range of 3.2 to 4 and a long, very ill-defined period; and R is a typical Mira star, with a range of 6 to 14 and a period of 370 days.

Close to η is M.35, a really splendid open cluster. It is visible to the naked eye as a dim patch, and it is well seen with binoculars. It is some 2,900 light-years away, and the diameter of the cluster is estimated at 30 light-years.

Taurus. The Bull. Only part of Taurus is shown here, but it includes β, or Alnath (magnitude 1.6) and ζ (3.1). Close to ζ is M.1, the Crab Nebula—the remnant of the supernova seen in 1054, and regarded by astro-physicists as one of the most informative objects in the sky. Small telescopes will show it as a faint blur.

Canis Minor. The Little Dog. The leading star, Procyon, is of magnitude 0.4; it is 5 times as luminous as the Sun, and at its distance of 10 light-years is the closest of all the bright stars apart from α Centauri and Sirius. It has a faint companion which is probably a white dwarf; however, large-aperture telescopes are needed to show it. Procyon is of spectral type F5, which means that it is slightly yellowish—though admittedly most observers would probably call it white.

The only other bright star in Canis Minor is β, of magnitude 2.9.

Monoceros. The Unicorn. This constellation also lies mainly south of the equator, but part of it appears on this chart. There are no bright stars, but Monoceros is crossed by the Milky Way, and so the whole area is rich enough to repay scanning with binoculars or a wide-field telescope. Some interesting telescopic objects do in fact exist, but all are inconveniently faint.

Orion. So far as these charts are concerned, it is unfortunate that the Celestial Hunter is sliced in two by the celestial equator, since it means that Orion is split between two. The whole constellation is shown on the chart on page 70. North of the equator we have Betelgeux and γ, or Bellatrix; Bellatrix is of magnitude 1.6, while Betelgeux is variable between about 0 and 1. Very occasionally Betelgeux may rival Rigel, but usually it is very slightly fainter than Procyon in the Little Dog. Aldebaran in Taurus is the most suitable comparison star, since it, too, is orange-red.

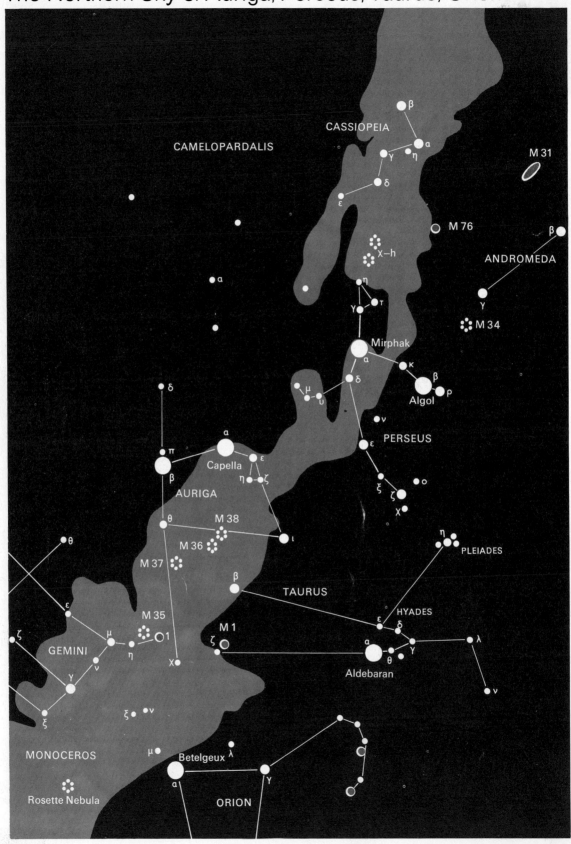

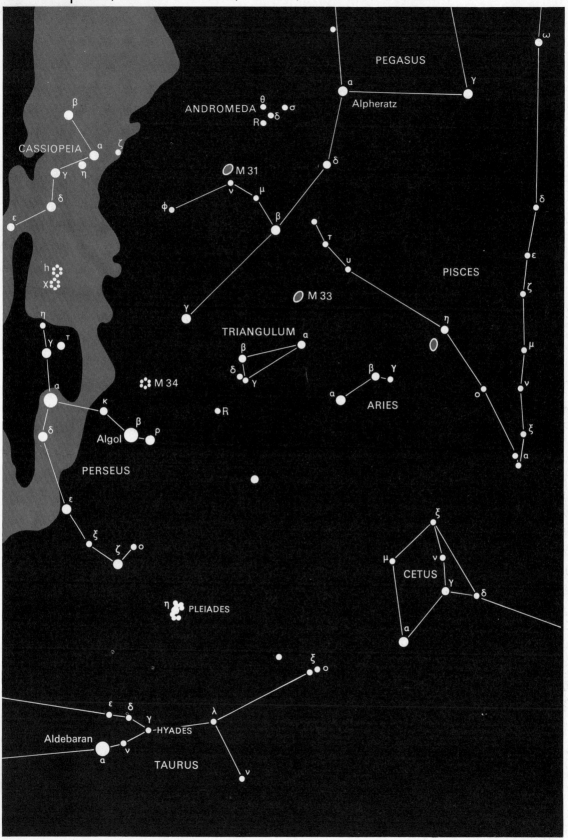

The Northern Sky 3: Notes

These charts include Auriga, with the brilliant Capella, together with the northernmost part of Orion. Also shown are Cassiopeia, with its famous W-shape; Perseus, which contains the celebrated eclipsing binary Algol; and Andromeda, in which lies the great galaxy M.31. There are only three stars of the first magnitude: Capella, Betelgeux, and Aldebaran. The Milky Way flows through Cassiopeia and Perseus past Gemini, so that all these constellations are extremely rich.

Cassiopeia. Cassiopeia resembles a W or an M. The four brightest stars of the W are α (Shedir) and γ, both of which are variable around the 2nd magnitude, δ (2.7) and ε (3.4).

Shedir is an orange star of spectral type K, and has a 9th-magnitude companion at a distance of 63"; this is an optical double, not a binary. Shedir itself has always been regarded as variable over a small range (about 2.1 to 2.5). The reality of the fluctuations has been questioned recently, and so Shedir is worth studying. Naked-eye comparisons can be made with β, which is definitely non-variable.

The central star of the W, γ, is variable, but it has no set period. Generally it is slightly fainter than the Pole Star, but occasionally it can brighten up to magnitude $1\frac{1}{2}$. It has a peculiar spectrum, and seems to be unstable.

There are several double stars in Cassiopeia; probably the finest is η, with magnitudes of 3.7 and 7.3 and a separation of 11".

If there is any difficulty in locating Cassiopeia, extend a line from Mizar in the Great Bear and pass it through Polaris, prolonging it for an equal distance beyond Polaris. However, Cassiopeia is so distinctive that it is recognizable at a glance. Over Great Britain it is circumpolar.

Andromeda. There are no 1st-magnitude stars here, but there are three of the second: β (2.0) and α and γ (2.1). Next comes δ, just below 3. α Andromedæ, often known by its proper name of Alpheratz, is included in the Square of Pegasus, and used to be called δ Pegasi. There seems no obvious reason for its transfer, because logically it belongs to the Pegasus pattern, whereas Andromeda is made up of a line of stars with no distinctive pattern at all.

The best way to locate Andromeda is to use the W of Cassiopeia. A line drawn from ε through δ, and continued, will lead to Alpheratz. The Andromeda chain can then be identified, stretching out towards Mirphak in Perseus and then on to Capella. Andromeda is not circumpolar from Britain, but it lies well to the north of the celestial equator, and is on view for much of the year. It is particularly well-placed during evenings in autumn.

γ Andromedæ (Almaak) is a fine double. The primary is of the 2nd magnitude, and the companion of the 5th; the separation is 9".8, so that this is a wide, easy pair. The contrasting colours are striking, since the bright star is orange and the companion bluish. The companion is itself a binary, with a period of 55 years. It was at its widest (0".6) in 1971, and has now started to close up. Under excellent conditions it can be split with an 8-in. telescope, but it is admittedly rather a difficult test. The other bright star in Andromeda, β (Mirach), is an M-type red giant; its colour comes out well when observed with binoculars.

The most notable variable star is R, which lies near the small triangle made up of θ, σ and ρ. It can become brighter than the 6th magnitude, and when near maximum it is on the fringe of naked-eye visibility; but at minimum it sinks down below magnitude 14, so that a fair-sized telescope is needed to show it.

The most famous object in Andromeda is the Great Spiral, M.31. It was known to the Arab astronomers of over a thousand years ago (Al-Sûfi, in A.D. 964, described it as 'a little cloud'), and it was examined telescopically as early as 1612 by Simon Marius, a contemporary and rival of Galileo. There are photographs of it on pages 9 and 45. The Spiral can be seen as a huge system, lying at an angle to us, and made up of stars; its distance is 2.2 million light-years, and it is the largest and most massive galaxy in our Local Group. It contains objects of all kinds, including nebulæ, galactic clusters and novæ; in the year 1885 a supernova in it (S Andromedæ) blazed forth and reached naked-eye visibility.

Yet one has to admit that to the amateur observer, M.31 is distinctly disappointing. On a clear night it is just visible with the naked eye, and binoculars show it clearly, but even with a large telescope it appears as nothing more than a blur of light.

The Great Spiral has two smaller companions, both of which are fairly easy objects. M.32 is a dwarf elliptical galaxy; so is the other companion, which was not listed by Messier but was included in Dreyer's New General Catalogue as NGC 205.

Pegasus. See pages 92 and 94.

Camelopardalis. See pages 85–6.

Perseus. This is a splendid constellation, whose pattern is easily recognized, crossed by the Milky Way and containing many objects of special interest. There is no 1st-magnitude star; the leader, α (Mirphak) is ranked 1.8. Then follow β (Algol), 2.1 at maximum; ζ, 2.8; γ and ε, 2.9; and δ, 3.0.

There are two double stars within the range of a small telescope. ζ has a companion of magnitude 9.4 at a distance of 12″.5; the primary is a luminous B-type supergiant. ε has an 8.3-magnitude companion at 9″.

The main interest of Perseus, as far as the amateur observer is concerned, is with its two bright variable stars and its clusters. Algol, or β Persei, is described on page 19. It is not a genuine variable, but an eclipsing binary; its behaviour was first explained in 1782 by John Goodricke. For most of the time it shines as a star of magnitude 2.1, so that it is practically as bright as the Pole Star. Every 2½ days it 'winks', taking 5 hours to fade down to magnitude 3.3; after a minimum lasting for 20 minutes, it spends a further 5 hours in returning to maximum. Its variations can be followed throughout with the naked eye.

Close to Algol is ρ Persei, which is a red semi-regular variable. Its range is between magnitudes 3.2 and 4.2; there is an excellent comparison star in κ (magnitude 4.0), on the opposite side of Algol. The fluctuations of ρ are not violent, and in general the magnitude is somewhere around 3.8. Like Algol, it can be followed with the naked eye.

Perseus contains a pair of spectacular open star-clusters. Strangely, they were not included in Messier's catalogue, but they were listed by Herschel, and are known as H.Vi. 33 and 34. They are visible with the naked eye, but are well seen only with optical aid. Binoculars show them excellently; there are twin clusters, side by side, each resolvable to its centre. With a low-power, wide-field eyepiece on a moderate-aperture telescope, the sight is beautiful. They form the Sword-Handle of Perseus (not to be confused with the gaseous nebula M.42, the Sword of Orion).

Also in the constellation is M.34, a large bright open cluster just north of a line joining Algol to γ Andromedæ; it is visible with the naked eye on a clear night. It contains well over a hundred stars, and is 1,450 light-years away from us.

Triangulum. The Triangle. Because of its shape, this little constellation is easy to identify, though its brightest star (β) is only of the 3rd magnitude. There is one typical Mira-type variable, R, which has a period of 266 days and is visible with binoculars at maximum; its range is from magnitude 6 to 12.

M.33, the Triangulum Spiral, is slightly more remote than the Andromeda Galaxy; it is also smaller, so that it is less conspicuous. There have been claims that keen-sighted people can see it with the naked eye, as a faint blur, under ideal conditions; certainly it is visible with binoculars, but it is of low surface brightness, and the slightest mist will obscure it. Look for it a little south of a line joining α Trianguli to β Andromedæ; but do not be surprised if you have considerable difficulty in picking it up. It is a loose spiral, but of course the structure is shown only on photographs taken with large telescopes.

Aries. The Ram. This is traditionally the first constellation of the Zodiac—though since the vernal equinox has now moved into Pisces, Aries should really come last in the order. It lies roughly between Aldebaran and the Square of Pegasus, and has one bright star: α (Hamal), magnitude 2.0. β (2.7) is also reasonably conspicuous. The most notable object is γ, which is a fine, easy double; the components are virtually equal at magnitude 4.7, and since they are over 8″ apart they are visible with any small telescope.

Pisces. The Fishes. One of the most obscure constellations in the Zodiac, though it covers a large area of the sky; it may be identified by the chain of faint stars running along south of the Square of Pegasus, but only one star in Pisces, η (3.7) is above the 4th magnitude. There are no telescopic objects of note. M.74 is a spiral galaxy, but it is not at all easy to pick up.

Auriga. See pages 85 and 86.

Gemini. See pages 85 and 87.

Taurus. The Bull. Here we have two important star-clusters, the Pleiades and the Hyades, as well as the Crab Nebula; there is also an eclipsing binary of the Algol type, λ, which varies between magnitudes 3.3 and 4.2 in a period of just under 4 days. The Pleiades, round η (Alcyone), have already been described; they make up the finest open cluster in the sky. The Hyades are more scattered, and are best seen with binoculars. As we have noted, Aldebaran is not a true member of the Hyades cluster, and lies approximately midway between the cluster and ourselves.

Orion. See pages 85 and 87.

Cetus. The Whale. Most of this very large constellation lies in the southern hemisphere; on the present chart we can see the Whale's head, in which α, or Menkar, a fine orange star of magnitude 2.5, is the leader.

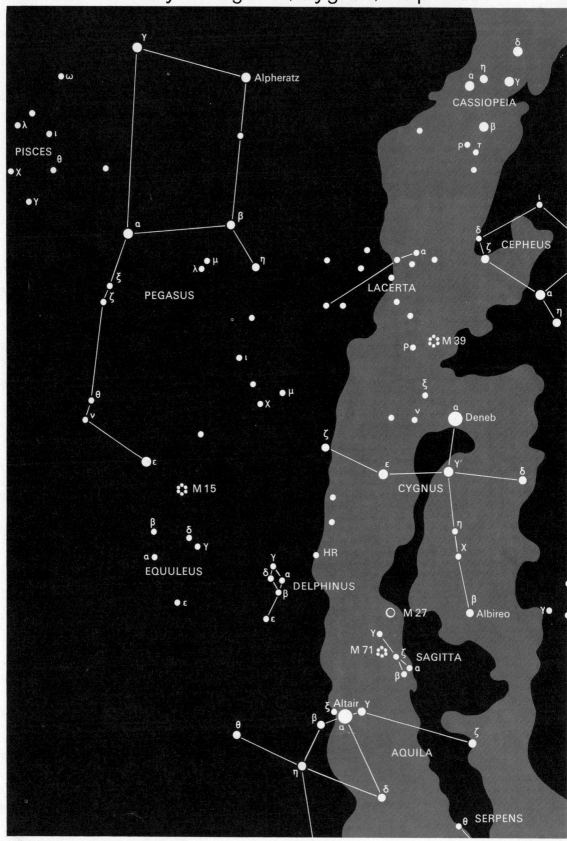

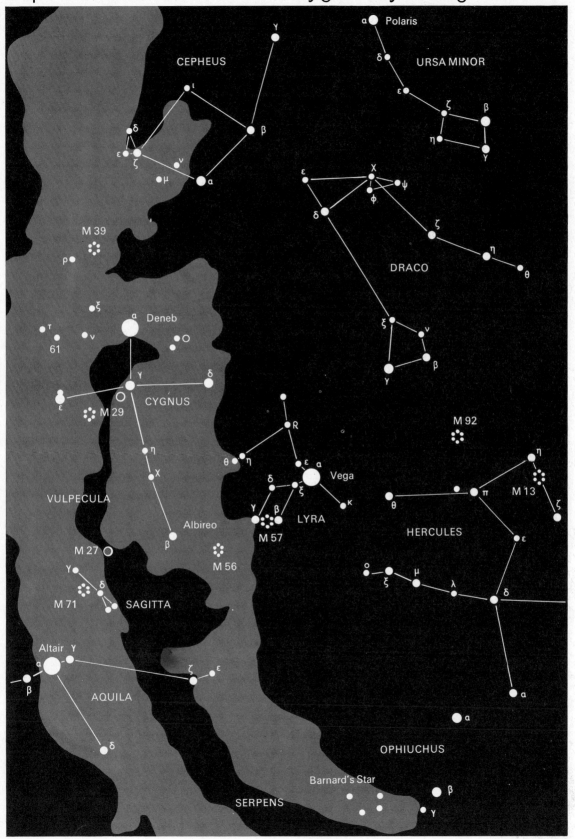

The Northern Sky 4: Notes

In these charts we have two constellations of exceptional interest: Cygnus (the Swan) and Pegasus. The 1st-magnitude stars are those making up the unofficial Summer Triangle: Vega, Altair and Deneb. The nickname was given because these brilliant stars dominate the summer evening sky in Great Britain, but they are winter objects to southern-hemisphere observers, and from countries such as Australia and South Africa they never rise high above the horizon.

Pegasus. This constellation, marked by its Square, dominates the evening sky in autumn over Europe. As we have noted, one star of the Square, Alpheratz, is now included in Andromeda. In Pegasus itself, the leaders are ε (2.3), α (2.5), β (variable from 2.4 to 2.8), η (2.8) and γ (2.9). β, or Scheat, is semi-regular with a rough period of about 35 days; it is visible as a huge red giant.

ε, or Enif, has been suspected of variability, though the evidence is not conclusive. Not far from it is a splendid globular cluster, M.15, with a bright, condensed centre; it lies in a rather barren area, and so is easy to find.

Lacerta. The Lizard. A very small and inconspicuous constellation between Pegasus and Cepheus. It contains nothing of note.

Cepheus. Not particularly conspicuous; there is only one star, α (2.4), above the 3rd magnitude. The best way to locate Cepheus is to continue the line from the pointers in Ursa Major through Polaris, and then look for the quadrilateral made up of β, α, ζ and ι. β is a double; magnitudes 3.3 and 8, separation 14″, so that it is an extremely wide and easy pair. In the same low-power binocular field as β is T Cephei, a long-period variable which ranges between magnitudes 5.5 and 9.6 in a mean period of 391 days.

However, the two chief variables in Cepheus are of much greater importance. δ is the typical short-period star, and has given the name 'Cepheid' to the entire class. It is of magnitude 3.5 at maximum and 4.4 at minimum; it forms a triangle with ζ (magnitude 3.3) and ε (4.2), which make useful comparisons. As the period is 5.4 days, the changes in brightness from one night to the next are quite noticeable, even though the overall range is less than a magnitude.

μ is quite different. It is probably the reddest star visible with the naked eye, although the colour does not show up without optical aid. Sir William Herschel aptly christened it the Garnet Star. It is an M-type giant, and if it were closer to us it would appear as imposing as Betelgeux. It is variable between magnitudes $3\frac{1}{2}$ and 5; there seems to be no semblance of a period, and ordinarily the fluctuations are slow. An excellent comparison star is ν, close by, which is of magnitude 4.5.

Ursa Minor. See pages 80 and 82.

Draco. See pages 80 and 82.

Cygnus. The Swan. It is easy to see why the constellation is often called the Northern Cross, and part of Cygnus, including Deneb, the leader, is circumpolar from Great Britain. Deneb is of magnitude 1.3; then come γ (2.2), ε (2.5) and δ (2.9). β, or Albireo (3.1), is the faintest member of the cross but it is a particularly beautiful double. The primary is golden yellow, and the 5th-magnitude companion is described by some observers as green and by others as blue. The separation is over 34″, so that even good binoculars will split the pair. I always regard it as the loveliest double in the whole sky. Should you have any difficulty in locating it, look for it slightly off a line joining Vega to Altair.

δ, also in the cross, is another double, but not nearly so imposing. The companion is of magnitude 6.5, and the separation is 2″; this is a binary, with a period of 321 years. Another binary, ζ (magnitudes 3.3 and 8; distance 2″.3) has a period of 500 years.

It is worth while locating a much fainter star, 61 Cygni, made up of two components, magnitudes 5.6 and 6.3, separation 28″. There is nothing striking about it, but it is notable as being the first star to have its distance measured. In 1838 F. W. Bessel, using the method of parallax, gave a value which was not very different from the true distance of 11.2 light-years. 61 Cygni is thus one of the closest stars to the Earth. Slight irregularities in the proper motion of the fainter component indicate that there is a third member in the system, which we cannot see; it may be a light-weight star, but is much more probably a massive planet.

Cygnus is exceptionally rich in variable stars. One of them, χ, is of the Mira type, and has the greatest range known; at its best it may become brighter than the 4th magnitude, but at minimum it drops to below the 14th. The period is 409 days. It is a powerful infra-red source; if our eyes were sensitive to infra-red radiation, χ Cygni would be one of the most brilliant stars in the sky. When near maximum, its neighbour, η (magnitude 4.0), is a useful comparison star.

Another star of the same type is R Cygni, with a period of 426 days and a range from magnitude 6 to below 14. It is very easy to locate, since it lies in the same telescopic field as the 4th-magnitude star θ Cygni. Also in the constellation we have one of the strange stars which may form a link between variables and novæ. This is P Cygni, near γ, which was first recorded in 1600, when it flared up from obscurity to the 3rd magnitude. It then declined, subsequently brightening once more to about the 5th magnitude, where it has remained ever since. It is very luminous and remote, and appears to be unstable; a few other similar stars are known, but P Cygni is the brightest of them, and is worth checking frequently just in case it shows signs of renewed activity.

Close to the fainter star Flamsteed 75, near ρ, is the irregular variable SS Cygni, which is normally of about the 12th magnitude, but which flares up to the 8th at intervals of about seven weeks. Like others of its kind it is a very close binary, one companion being of solar type, the other a white dwarf.

Cygnus is crossed by the Milky Way; we have here not only rich star-fields but also the dark rifts due to obscuring material. No galaxies can be made out, because they are hidden by the intervening dust and gas lying along the main plane of our own Galaxy; but there are some open clusters. M.39, near ρ, is visible with the naked eye, and is impressive in binoculars; M.29, not far from γ, contains some fairly bright stars, but is much less condensed.

Lyra. See pages 80 and 82.

Equuleus. The Foal. A very small and faint constellation near Delphinus; it contains nothing of note.

Delphinus. The Dolphin. Though there is no star brighter than β (magnitude 3.7), Delphinus can hardly be mistaken, because it is so compact. One of the stars in its main pattern, γ, is double; magnitudes 4.5 and 5.5, separation 10″.5. The primary is yellowish and the companion bluish-green, although the colours are not particularly striking.

It was in Delphinus that G. E. D. Alcock, in 1967, discovered the nova which is now called HR Delphini. It was visible to the naked eye, and brightened up to above the 4th magnitude; it was slow to fade, and is in every way an exceptional object. By mid-1973 it had still not faded down to magnitude $10\frac{1}{2}$. Before its outburst the magnitude was 12, and it may be expected to return to its old state, so that it will stay within the range of small telescopes.

Vulpecula. The Fox. The Dumbbell Nebula, M.27, is the one important telescopic object here. It was discovered by Messier in 1764, and is by no means a difficult object; the nearest naked-eye star is γ Sagittæ, three degrees to the south. Though the details are well seen only by means of photography, M.27 shows considerable structure when observed with a telescope of fair aperture; it is much less symmetrical than the Ring Nebula in Lyra. Its estimated distance is 975 light-years.

Sagitta. The Arrow. The brightest stars (δ and γ) are only just above the 4th magnitude, but the compact shape of Sagitta makes it easy to locate. It lies in the region between β Cygni and Altair. The most interesting telescopic object is M.71, a 9th-magnitude globular which will be found between δ and γ. It is less regular and condensed than some globulars, but is quite an impressive sight.

Aquila. The Eagle. Here again we have a constellation which is cut by the celestial equator, but the leading star, Altair, is well inside the northern hemisphere of the sky. Altair, with a magnitude of 0.8, is the twelfth brightest star in the sky; it is considerably inferior to Vega, but much more brilliant than Deneb. Appearances are deceptive; Altair is only 9 times more luminous than the Sun, whereas Deneb is equal to at least 10,000 Suns. At its distance of 16 light-years, Altair is one of the nearest of the 1st-magnitude stars.

The other leading stars of Aquila are γ (2.7) and ζ (3.0). γ, or Tarazed, is decidedly reddish in hue. It lies to one side of Altair; the star on the other side, β, is only just above the 4th magnitude.

South of Altair may be seen a line of three stars: θ, η and δ. The central member, η, is a Cepheid variable with a range from 3.7 to 4.5 and a period of 7.2 days. It is easy to follow with binoculars; suitable comparisons are δ (3.4) and β (3.9), η Aquilæ appears with almost the same brightness as δ Cephei, described above; but it has a longer period, and so is more luminous and more remote.

Serpens. Adjoining Aquila is the body of Serpens (Cauda), which extends across the equator. Near δ Aquilæ is the very fine double Alya, or θ Serpentis. Here the companions are exactly equal at magnitude 4.5, and the separation is 22″, so that this is one of the easiest pairs of 'twins' in the sky. To find it, simply continue the line of θ, η, and δ Auilæ.

Hercules. See pages 80 and 83.

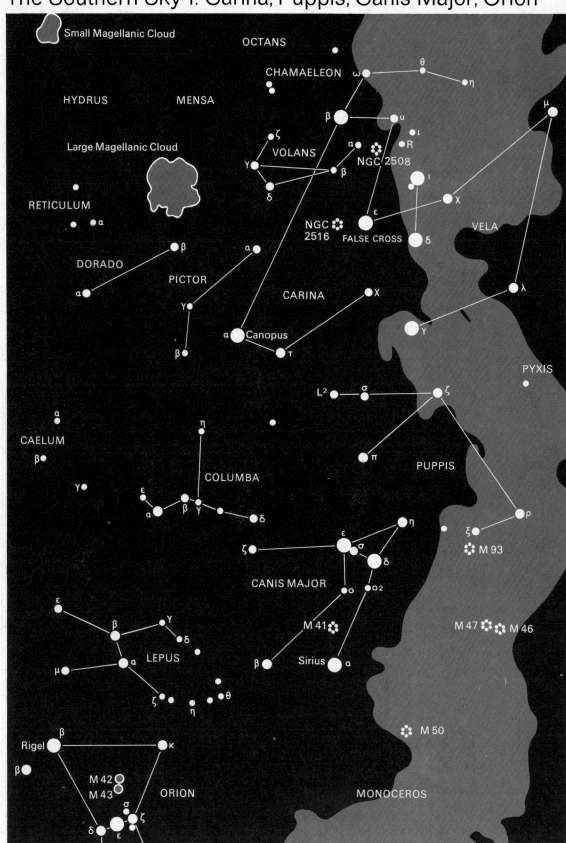

Vela, Puppis, Crater, Hydra

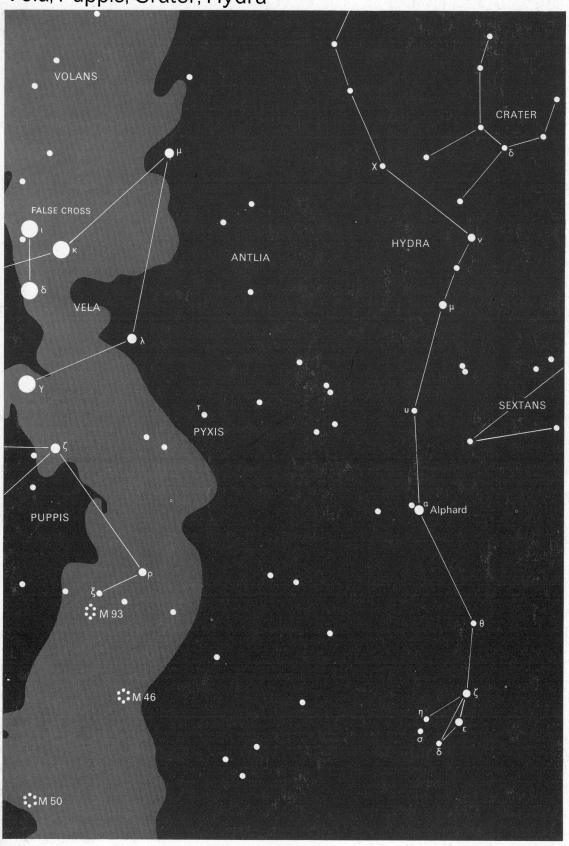

VOLANS

FALSE CROSS
ι
κ

δ

VELA

λ

γ

τ

PYXIS

ζ

PUPPIS

ρ

ξ

M 93

M 46

M 50

ANTLIA

HYDRA

χ

ν

μ

υ

α Alphard

SEXTANS

CRATER

δ

θ

ζ

η

σ

ε

δ

The Southern Sky 1: Notes

Much of these charts is occupied by the old constellation of Argo Navis, the Ship Argo. This huge group was, in fact, so large that astronomers came to regard it as unwieldy, and cut it up into a keel, sails, a poop and a compass. Canopus, the second brightest star in the sky, was included in Carina, the Keel; here too is the extraordinary, erratic variable which was formerly called η Argûs and has now become η Carinæ.

Both the Clouds of Magellan are also shown, together with the 1st-magnitude stars Sirius and Rigel. On the other hand there are vast barren areas: Hydra, Antlia, Sextans and Crater have only one bright star between them.

Chamæleon. The Chameleon. One of the very obscure constellations in the south polar area; there is no star as bright as the 4th magnitude.

Pictor. The Painter. A small constellation not far from Canopus; its brightest star, α, is rather below the 3rd magnitude. In 1925 a bright nova, RR Pictoris, appeared in this region, and reached the 1st magnitude before fading away. It is now a very dim telescopic object, beyond the range of amateur-owned instruments.

Volans. The Flying Fish (originally Piscis Volans). This is a small constellation which intrudes into Carina; there seems no reason for it to have a separate identity. The brightest stars, β and ζ, are only just above the 4th magnitude. γ is a wide, easy double; magnitudes 4 and 5.8, separation almost 14″.

Carina. The Keel (of Argo). Undoubtedly this is the most interesting part of the Ship, as well as being the most brilliant. The dominant star is Canopus, of magnitude −0.7; it is inferior only to Sirius in apparent brightness, and is very much more luminous. Estimates differ, but according to some authorities Canopus is the equal of 80,000 Suns put together, in which case it is more powerful even than Rigel. The spectral type is F, and so Canopus should be yellowish; but to me it appears pure white, whether I look at it with the naked eye, with binoculars or with a telescope.

The other leading stars in Carina are ε (1.7), β (1.8), ι (2.2), and θ (3.0). ε and ι make up the False Cross, together with δ and κ Velorum. Three are hot and white, but ε is a beautiful orange star of spectral type K.

υ Carinæ is double; magnitudes 3 and 6, separation 4″.6. It lies not far from β, sometimes known by its proper name of Miaplacidus.

Of the variable stars in Carina, much the most remarkable is η, which is possibly the most erratic object in the sky. During the 1830s it became extremely brilliant, and at its peak, in the late 1830s and early 1840s, it outshone even Canopus. After 1843 it began to fade, and for almost a century now it has been invisible with the naked eye, though binoculars show it clearly.

η Carinæ is not an ordinary variable; neither can it be classed as a nova, though admittedly it does have some nova-like characteristics. Its mass seems to be about 80 times that of the Sun, which is exceptionally great, and it is also very luminous; the distance is generally taken to be rather over 6,000 light-years. The star is involved in nebulosity, and is certainly unstable. For a long time now there have been no marked changes in brightness, but we never know when η Carinæ may undergo another outburst, so that it is always worth watching.

R Carinæ is a variable of different type; it is of the Mira class, and ranges between 3.9 and 10 in a period of 309 days. Near it is l, which is a Cepheid; the magnitude changes between 3.6 and 5, and the period is 35.5 days. The Cepheid law states 'the longer the period, the more powerful the star', so that l Carinæ is very luminous indeed; for comparison the period of δ Cephei, is only just over 5 days.

Carina is very well supplied with rich starfields. There are also some bright clusters; NGC 2516, near ε, is visible with the naked eye, while NGC 2808, near ι and υ, is a globular. Of course, nebulous objects in Carina do not have Messier numbers; they never rise above the horizon from France, where Charles Messier carried out all his observational work.

Vela. The Sails (of Argo). With Carina, this is the brightest part of the Ship. There are five stars above the 3rd magnitude: γ (1.9), δ (2.0), λ (2.2), κ (2.6) and μ (2.8), together with several more above the 4th; the area is very rich.

Two of the stars in Vela, δ and κ, make up a cross pattern with ε and ι Carinæ. This is known as the False Cross, and unwary observers have been known to confuse it with the Southern Cross, Crux Australis; but there is no excuse for this, because the False Cross is so much larger and fainter.

γ is the brightest of the so-called Wolf-Rayet stars; it has a companion of magnitude 4.8, and since the separation is over 40″ this is an exceptionally wide and easy pair. Wolf-Rayet stars are unstable, and have very high surface temperatures. Their spectra show emission lines, indicating that they have very extended atmospheres.

δ has a companion of magnitude 6.5, at a distance of 2″.9; μ is a much closer double, though the companion is of the 7th magnitude and the pair is not a particularly difficult test for a 6-inch telescope.

There are no really important variables in Vela, but the reddish star N, near κ, in the False Cross, is worth watching with binoculars, since there is some doubt as to whether it is variable or not.

No part of Vela can be seen from Great Britain.

Antlia. The Air-pump; originally Antlia Pneumatica, a name which astronomers wisely decided to abbreviate. It lies between Hydra and Vela; there is no star brighter than magnitude $4\frac{1}{2}$, and there are no telescopic objects of any interest at all.

Crater. The Cup. The guide-star to Crater is ν Hydræ, of the 3rd magnitude; Crater itself contains nothing brighter than magnitude 3.8.

Columba. The Dove; originally Columba Noachi, Noah's Dove. An unremarkable constellation with only one star above the 3rd magnitude (α, 2.6). Look for it some way off the line joining Sirius to Canopus. It is always very low from England, and the southernmost star in its pattern (η) never rises; but from Australia and South Africa it can reach the zenith, as happens during evenings in February and March (the southern-hemisphere autumn).

Puppis. The Poop (of Argo). This is the northernmost part of Argo, and part of it can be seen from Britain, though it is always very low. The principal stars are ζ (2.3), π (2.7) and ρ (2.9). ζ is another very hot star of spectral type O. σ is double; magnitudes 3.2 and 8.5, separation 22″.4.

Not far from σ is L², which is a semi-regular variable ideally suited for observation with binoculars. The maximum range is from 2.6 to 6; σ makes a suitable comparison star, together with L, which is visible very close to L² and is of magnitude 5.0.

The open cluster M.46 lies in Puppis; its declination is only −14°42′, so that it can attain a respectable height above the British horizon. The distance from us is over 3,000 light-years, according to the Swedish astronomer Wallenquist, who gives the diameter of the cluster as 26 light-years. Close beside it is another cluster, M.47, which is rather brighter, and is just visible with the naked eye; Wallenquist's measurements indicate that it

is closer to us than M.46, and lies at 1,750 light years distance.

Pyxis. The Compass; part of the old Argo, but a very small and unimportant portion, with no star above magnitude 3.7. T Pyxidis is a recurrent nova; normally it is very faint, but in 1920 and again in 1944 it rose briefly to the 7th magnitude. It is therefore of the same general glass as T Coronæ Borealis, the Blaze Star, in the northern hemisphere, but is much less spectacular.

Hydra. The Watersnake. Alphard, of magnitude 2.0, lies in line with Castor and Pollux, which is probably the best way to identify it. It is decidedly reddish, and is very much on its own; it is indeed called the Solitary One.

Canis Major. The Great Dog. This constellation —and indeed the whole area—is dominated by Sirius, which so obviously outshines any other star in the sky. Europeans do not see it to full advantage; from Britain it is always rather low down, and seems to flash all the colours of the rainbow even though it is really a pure white star of spectral type A. Go to a southern-hemisphere country, such as Australia or South Africa, and you will be able to appreciate the full glory of Sirius riding high in the sky. It always twinkles, but it is steadier than as seen from the north, and it is a superb sight. Yet, as we have noted, Sirius is one of the least luminous of the 1st-magnitude stars, and has a candle-power only 26 times that of the Sun. At a distance of 8.6 light-years, it is exceptionally close to us on the overall scale of the universe.

The white dwarf companion is by no means faint, and but for the proximity of the brilliant primary it would be easily seen in binoculars; but it is so overpowered that it is not visible in small telescopes. To show it, the best method is to block out Sirius itself by means of an occulting bar in the telescope eyepiece.

Canis Major contains other bright stars: ε (1.6), δ (1.8), β (2.0), η (2.5) and ζ and o² (3.0). All these are much more powerful than Sirius, but also much more remote. There are not many interesting telescopic objects in the constellation apart from the open cluster M.41, which is visible to the naked eye when high up.

Monoceros. A part of the Unicorn appears on this chart, adjoining Puppis and Canis Major; but apart from the galactic cluster M.50 there is nothing in it of special note.

Orion, Lepus, Cælum, Dorado, Reticulum, Mensa and Hydrus are described on pages 110–1. Octans is described on page 106.

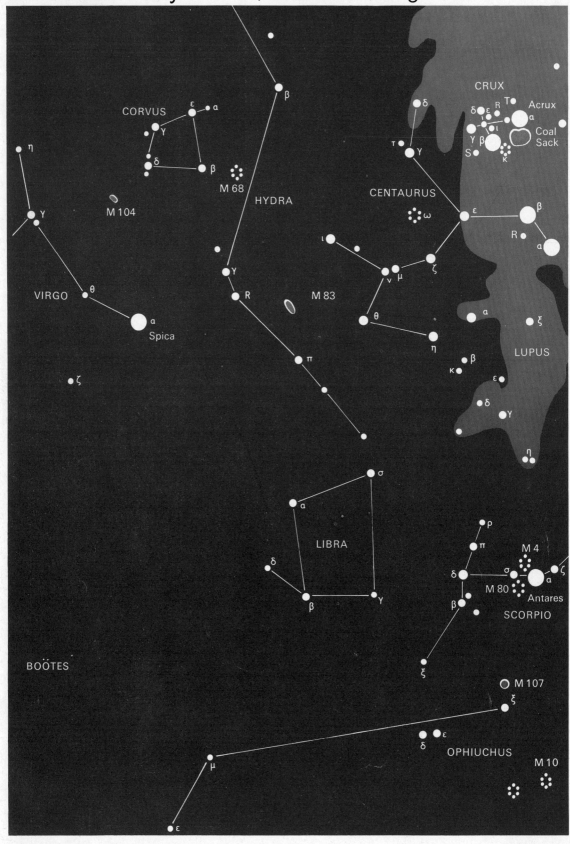

Crux, Lupus, Ara, Scorpio, Sagittarius

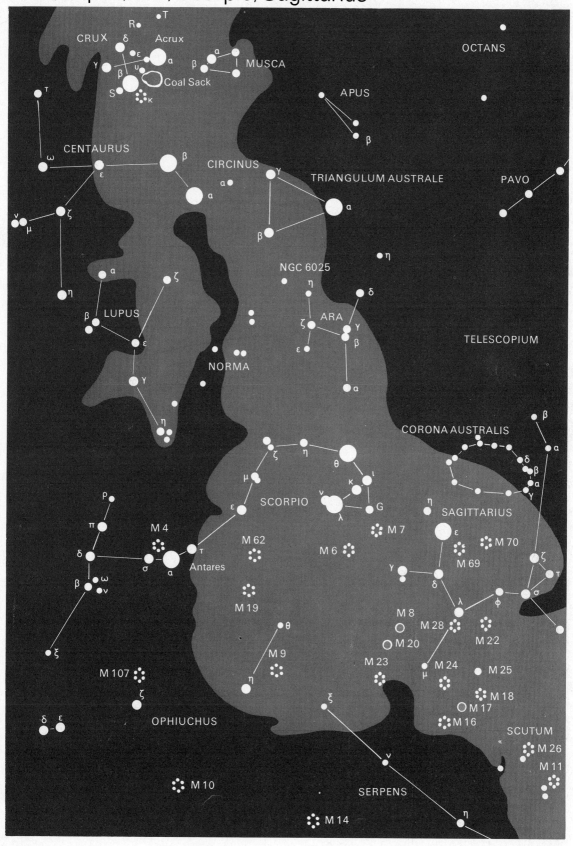

The Southern Sky 2: Notes

Several large and important constellations are included in these maps. Scorpio is one of the brightest groups in the entire sky and is also one of the most distinctive. Unfortunately, it is never well seen from European latitudes. Sagittarius adjoins it, and is described on page 107. We have also Crux Australis, the Southern Cross, and the two pointers in Centaurus, completing a truly glorious region. The Milky Way is particularly rich in this part of the sky, and in the direction of the Sagittarius star-clouds we are looking towards the centre of the Galaxy.

Virgo. The Virgin. In this part of Virgo we find the leading star, the 1st-magnitude Spica, as well as the binary γ or Arich. The components of Arich are equal at magnitude $3\frac{1}{2}$; the period is 172 years. The separation is becoming steadily less and less, and in half a century the star will appear single in all but large telescopes.

Corvus. The Crow. Europeans do not appreciate that this constellation, with its well-marked quadrilateral, can be very prominent when high in the sky. There are four fairly bright stars: γ (2.6), β (2.7), δ (3.0) and ε (also 3.0). There is nothing of telescopic interest, however.

Hydra. The Watersnake. In this section of the constellation lies the long-period variable R Hydræ, near γ. This is of the Mira type, and has a period of 415 days; the range is from magnitude 4 to 10, so that it is one of the brightest members of its class.

M.68, near the boundary of Hydra with Corvus, is a globular cluster. M.83 is a spiral galaxy, very similar in size and luminosity to our own Galaxy; but at its distance of over 8 million light-years it is not conspicuous, and the fact that there are no bright stars near it makes it difficult to locate.

Centaurus. The Centaur. A splendid constellation, containing bright stars, doubles, variables and clusters—including ω, the finest globular in the entire sky.

The two leaders of Centaurus, α and β, are of magnitudes -0.3 and $+0.7$ respectively, and form the pointers to the Southern Cross. Next in order of brightness come θ (2.2), γ (2.3), η (2.6), ε (2.6), ι (2.9), δ (2.9) and ζ (3.0). The pattern is unmistakable, and of course the pointers make the constellation instantly recognizable.

α Centauri is the nearest star in the sky—or, rather, the nearest star-group; the closest member, the dim red dwarf Proxima, is officially known as

α Centauri C, and is about a tenth of a light-year nearer to us than the bright pair. α itself is a fine binary with a period of 80 years; the magnitudes of the components are 0.3 and 1.7, so that there is a considerable difference between them. Both separation and position angle alter fairly rapidly, but the pair can always be split with a small telescope.

Close to the pointers is a Mira-type variable, R Centauri, which has a range from magnitude 5.4 to 11.8, and the long period of 547 days.

Of the nebulæ and clusters, two objects are worthy of special mention. The peculiar galaxy Centaurus A is a radio source, once—though not now—believed to be a pair of colliding galaxies; it lies far beyond our Milky Way, and is optically faint. On the other hand, the globular cluster ω Centauri is very conspicuous even with the naked eye. Binoculars will resolve the outer parts of it, and in a telescope it is a superb sight, far outclassing M.13 Herculis, the brightest globular of the northern sky.

Crux Australis. There can be few Australians, New Zealanders or South Africans who cannot recognize the Southern Cross. The four bright stars, so close together, are striking, and cannot possibly be overlooked. Two are ranked of the first magnitude: α (Acrux) (0.9) and β (1.3); then come γ (1.6) and δ (3.1). There is also ε (3.6), which tends to spoil the symmetry.

Acrux is a wide, easy double; the components are of magnitudes 1.6 and 2.1, and are $4''.7$ apart, so that any telescope will split them. There is also a third star in the field. γ has a 6.7-magnitude companion at $111''$; this is not a binary, but an optical pair.

It is instructive to take a pair of binoculars and look at the four main stars of the Cross in turn. Three of them are hot and white. The fourth, γ, is of spectral type M, and is a lovely orange-red.

There are three Cepheid variables in the constellation: R, S and T, all of which have ranges between magnitudes 6 and 8 and periods between $4\frac{3}{4}$ and $6\frac{3}{4}$ days. However, the most interesting objects, apart from the stars of the Cross themselves, are the Jewel Box and the Coal Sack. The Coal Sack has already been described; it is a dark nebula close to Acrux and β. The Jewel Box is the nickname given to the bright cluster round κ Crucis, because in it there are stars of various colours.

Musca Australis. The Southern Fly, often called simply Musca. A compact little constellation near Acrux; the brightest star is α, magnitude 2.9. β is double; the components are almost equal (magnitude 4) and 1″.6 apart.

Circinus. The Compasses. A small constellation near the pointers. The leading star, α (magnitude 3.4) is yellowish, and has an 8.8-magnitude companion at 15″.8.

Triangulum Australe. See pages 104 and 106.

Lupus. The Wolf. This constellation occupies the area between Scorpio and Centaurus, and contains several fairly bright stars, of which the chief are β (2.8), α (2.9) and γ (also 2.9). There is no distinctive shape, and this makes Lupus rather hard to identify. Neither are there any particularly notable objects, although κ, near β, is a very wide and easy double; magnitudes 4.1 and 6, separation 27″. η, of magnitude 3.6, has a 7.7-magnitude companion at 15″, so that this pair also is well within the range of almost any telescope.

In 1006 a supernova appeared in Lupus. We know little about it, but from the fragmentary records it seems to have become a naked-eye object in broad daylight. It has been associated with a radio source in the corresponding position.

Norma. The Rule. A very obscure constellation, with no star as bright as the 4th magnitude.

Ara. See pages 104 and 106.

Libra. The Scales or Balance. This is the least interesting of the Zodiacal groups; there are two stars above the 3rd magnitude, β (2.6) and α (2.8). The next star in order of brightness, σ, is of magnitude 3.3, and used to be included in Scorpio; it was then called γ Scorpionis.

The only object of any real interest to the amateur observer is δ, which is an Algol-type eclipsing binary with a period of 2.3 days and a range of magnitude from 4.8 to 6.2.

Scorpio. The Scorpion. The Latin name is often (perhaps more correctly) given as Scorpius. The whole of the constellation can be seen from latitudes to the south of Europe, though from Britain the Sting never rises. From Australia and South Africa the Scorpion can pass overhead, and cannot be mistaken. The leading stars are α, or Antares, (1.0), λ, or Shaula, (1.6), θ, or Sargas, (1.9), δ (2.3), ε (2.3), κ (2.4), β (2.6), υ (2.7), σ (2.8), τ (2.8), and π (2.9)—an impressive list. σ and τ lie to either side of Antares.

Antares, probably the reddest of all the bright stars, is a beautiful object, particularly when observed with binoculars. It is a huge supergiant, with a diameter of over 200 million miles. At 3″

from it is the companion, which is of the 5th magnitude and would be visible with the naked eye were it not so overpowered. The green colour of the small star is due largely to contrast with the primary, but is very marked, and many people consider that Antares rivals β Cygni as the most impressive double star in the sky.

Two more double stars lie in the Scorpion's head. ν is very wide and easy; the magnitudes are 4.3 and 6.5, and the separation is 41″. Each component is again double, but very close and difficult. The nearby β, of magnitude 2.8, has a 5th-magnitude companion at 1″, and there is another 5th-magnitude star at 14″.

In the sting there are two bright stars close together. λ, or Shaula, is only just too faint to be ranked with the 1st-magnitude stars. Its neighbour, υ or Lesath, is of almost exactly the same luminosity, and it seems much less conspicuous only because it is further away; about 540 light-years, as against 310 for Shaula.

Of the many star-clusters in Scorpio, one of the easiest to find is M.4, which is only 1½ degrees away from Antares. It is quite bright, and is a globular cluster at the small distance of 7,500 light-years from us. M.80 is also a globular, though not so bright; to find it, look almost midway between Antares and β. In 1860 a bright nova appeared in it, and completely outshone the cluster for a week or two, though it has long since faded into invisibility.

Of the open clusters, M.6 and M.7 are among the finest. They lie in the southern part of the constellation, near the sting, and are thus not well seen from Europe or the northern United States, but as seen from Australia or South Africa they are easily visible with the naked eye. M.7 is the larger of the two, and is most spectacular when observed through good binoculars or a finder; with higher powers it more than covers the entire field of the telescope.

Corona Australis. See pages 104 and 107.

Ophiuchus. Much of this very large constellation lies in the southern hemisphere, and is shown on this chart, though the brightest star, α or Rasalgethi, is in the north (close to α Herculis). Of the stars shown here, three are above the third magnitude: η (2.5), ζ (2.6) and δ (2.7).

Despite its size, Ophiuchus is rather barren, and there are no noteworthy double stars or variables; but there are several fairly bright globular clusters, of which M.10, M.9 and M.19 are easy to find.

Serpens. See pages 104 and 107.

Sagittarius. See pages 104 and 107.

The Southern Sky 3: Pavo, Ara, Sagittarius

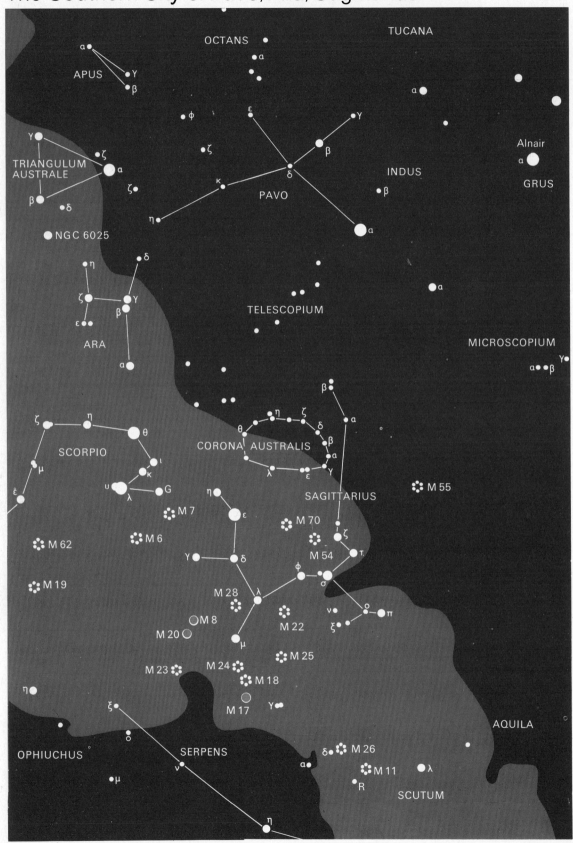

Indus, Grus, Capricornus, Aquarius

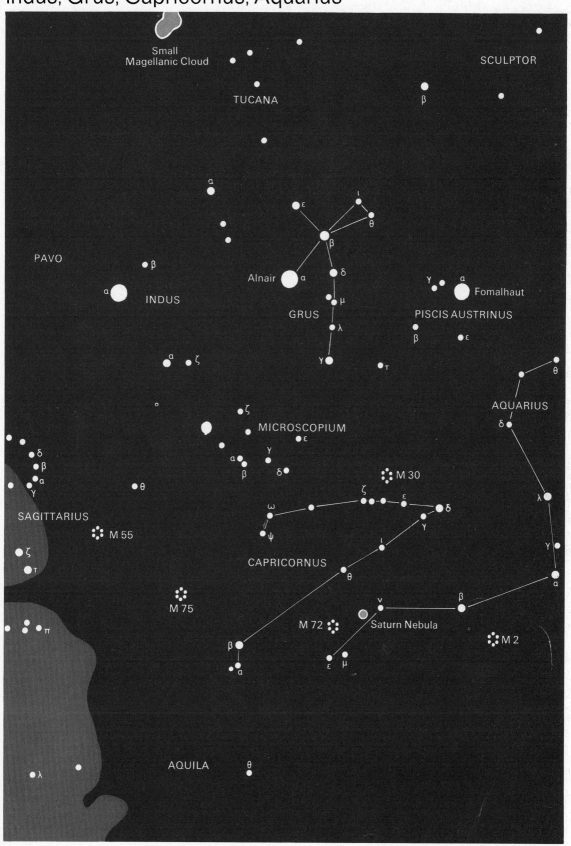

The Southern Sky 3: Notes

These charts include some of the richest and some of the poorest areas in the sky. Looking towards the magnificent star-clouds in Sagittarius, we are seeing the direction of the centre of the Galaxy; on the other hand Capricornus, Aquarius and Sculptor are faint and barren.

Apus. The Bee. A fairly compact constellation, but with only two stars above the 4th magnitude.

Octans. The Octant. This, the south polar constellation, extends over this and the next pair of charts. The only star in it to exceed the fourth magnitude is ν (3.7), and there is nothing here to interest telescopic observers. Octans would be entirely unremarkable but for the fact that it does contain the pole; the nearest star to the polar point is σ, of magnitude 5.5.

Tucana. See pages 109 and 110.

Grus. The Crane. This is much the most distinctive of the Southern Birds, and it is not hard to picture a flying bird. The leaders, α (Alnair) (magnitude 2.1) and β (2.2) are very different; Alnair is bluish-white, while β is a beautiful orange colour. In the line of stars extending from β to the 3rd-magnitude γ there are two pairs, δ and μ, which are easy to separate with the naked eye; but both are too wide to be classed as proper doubles. From Australia or South Africa, Grus is almost overhead during evenings in spring (October).

Sculptor. Part of this very faint constellation lies on the chart, but there is nothing of interest to the amateur observer.

Piscis Austrinus. The Southern Fish. Fomalhaut, of the first magnitude, is always easy to recognize, since it lies in so barren an area; Piscis Austrinus contains no other star above the 4th magnitude. From Europe, Fomalhaut is always low (from North Scotland it barely rises at all), and only when it is seen from southern countries does the observer realize how bright it really is. At a distance of 24 light-years, it is one of our near neighbours, and is 13 times as luminous as the Sun.

Triangulum Australe. The Southern Triangle. A distinctive constellation which contains one bright star: α (1.9). The other two members of the triangle, β and γ, are of the third magnitude.

Triangulum Australe lies close to α Centauri,

which is shown on the previous chart. Its leader, α, is red; the colour is evident even with the naked eye, and is striking in binoculars.

There are no really notable doubles or variables, but there is one open cluster, NGC 6025, which is distinctly visible with the naked eye on a clear night.

Pavo. The Peacock. This is one of the Southern Birds; the others are Grus (the Crane), Tucana (the Toucan) and Phoenix (the Phoenix).

Pavo contains one bright star, α, which is of magnitude 2.1. There are no others above magnitude $3\frac{1}{2}$. I have always found that this area is one of the most confusing in the sky, and one needs an anchor to sort it out; one of the best methods is to find α Pavonis by extending a line from α Centauri through α Trianguli Australis and continuing it. α Pavonis will be found without much trouble, because there are no bright stars anywhere near it.

The main object of note in Pavo is κ, which is a typical Cepheid variable. Its range is from 4 to 5.5, and its period is 9.1 days; since this is longer than the periods of the two brightest Cepheids visible from Europe (δ Cephei itself and η Aquilæ), κ Pavonis is clearly the more luminous. Its fluctuations can be followed with the naked eye.

It is worth looking at δ, which is of magnitude 3.6. It is 19 light-years from us, and is a star remarkably similar to the Sun in size, mass and luminosity. Whether it has a family of planets must remain a matter for speculation, but there seems no reason why not. To an observer living in that system, the Sun would appear very much as δ Pavonis does to us.

Indus. The Indian. A small and quite unremarkable constellation near α Pavonis. Its brightest star is just below the 3rd magnitude.

Ara. The Altar. Like Lupus, Ara contains a fair number of brightish stars, but has few interesting objects. The leaders are β (2.8) and α and ζ, which are just about the 3rd magnitude. Ara is not difficult to find, since it lies between Triangulum Australe and Scorpio.

Telescopium. Another small, uninteresting constellation near Pavo, with no star brighter than magnitude 3.8. There is really no reason for it to have a separate identity.

Microscopium. The Microscope. An entirely obscure constellation adjoining Indus.

Scorpio. See pages 101 and 103.

Corona Australis. The Southern Crown. A small circlet of stars, by no means as conspicuous as Corona Borealis, but worthy of being ranked as a separate constellation; it lies near the comparatively faint stars α and β Sagittarii. γ is double; the components are almost equal at magnitude 5, and the separation is 2″.7, so that the pair is easy to split.

Sagittarius. The Archer. A large, bright constellation; there is no star of the first magnitude, but there are half a dozen above the third— ε (1.8), σ (2.1), ζ (2.6), δ (2.7), λ (2.8), and π (2.9). Curiously, both α and β are much fainter. Sagittarius is the southernmost constellation of the Zodiac, and so is never well seen from Europe, but from Australia and South Africa it is very prominent. During evenings in August and September it is almost overhead.

There are relatively few important doubles and variables in the constellation, but Sagittarius contains a remarkable number of nebulous objects bright enough to have been listed by Messier. They are as follows:

OBJECT	INTEGRATED MAGNITUDE
M.8, the Lagoon Nebula	6
M.17, the Omega or Horsehoe Nebula	7
M.20, the Trifid Nebula	9
M.21, an open cluster	6.5
M.22, a globular cluster	6
M.23, an open cluster	7
M.24, an open cluster	4.6
M.25, an open cluster	6.5
M.28, a globular cluster	7
M.54, a globular cluster	7
M.55, a globular cluster	7.6
M.69, a globular cluster	9
M.70, a globular cluster	9.6
M.75, a globular cluster	8

Note that there is not one galaxy. This is understandable, since any galaxy in this direction would lie beyond the centre of our own system, and would be very effectively hidden by the interstellar matter in the main plane of the Milky Way. On the other hand there are several globular clusters, while the first three objects in the list (M.8, 17 and 20) are gaseous nebulæ.

Some of these objects have already been described. Most of them are fairly easy to locate, for an observer in the southern hemisphere; to Europeans, Sagittarius is always inconveniently low.

M.8, the Lagoon Nebula, is faintly visible with the naked eye, though I always find some difficulty in seeing it without optical aid. The open cluster M.24 is much brighter, and looks rather like a detached portion of the Milky Way. M.22 is a particularly fine globular; it is almost as bright as M.13 Herculis, and is looser, so that it is easier to resolve.

The whole of Sagittarius will well repay examination with binoculars or a rich-field telescope.

Capricornus. The Sea-goat. This is a Zodiacal group, but not a bright one; its two chief stars, δ and β, are only of magnitude 2.9. α is a naked-eye double; the components are of magnitudes 3.7 and 4.3, and the distance is 376″. The fainter component is itself a double, but the companion, at 7″ distance, is only of the 11th magnitude. β is another very wide double; magnitudes 3 and 6, distance 205″; and again the fainter component is a double. The companion is of magnitude 10.6, but is only at a separation of 1″.3.

There are two globular clusters in Capricornus (M.30 and M.72) but both are rather faint.

Aquarius. The Water-bearer. Another large but dim Zodiacal constellation. The chief stars are β (2.9) and α (3.0), and, as with Capricornus, there is no distinctive pattern. There are, however, a few objects worthy of mention. ζ is a fine binary with almost equal components (magnitudes 4.4 and 4.6) and a separation of just under 2″; the period is 360 years. M.2, between β Aquarii and ε Pegasi, is a magnificent globular, which is easy to resolve with a moderate telescope. There is also the Saturn Nebula, H.VI.1, in the same low-power field as the orange star ν, which is a particularly bright planetary nebula, well worth finding.

Serpens. Cauda (the Body) appears on this chart. The brightest star in it is η, slightly below the 3rd magnitude; but the only notable object, the fine double, θ, is just north of the celestial equator, shown on page 93.

Scutum. The Shield. A small group lying close to λ Aquilæ, which is the best guide to it. There is no star as bright as the 4th magnitude, but the constellation is in the midst of the Milky Way, and there are some fine star-fields in it as well as two notable clusters. M.11, nicknamed the Wild Duck, is particularly beautiful, and is just visible with the naked eye. The densest part of the cluster is fan-shaped, with a star of the 8th magnitude just inside the point of the fan; when seen with an adequate telescope it really does conjure up the impression of a bird in flight. The cluster is 5,500 light-years away, and contains over 600 stars above the 15th magnitude, so that it is exceptionally rich. The other open cluster in Scutum, M.26, is much less impressive.

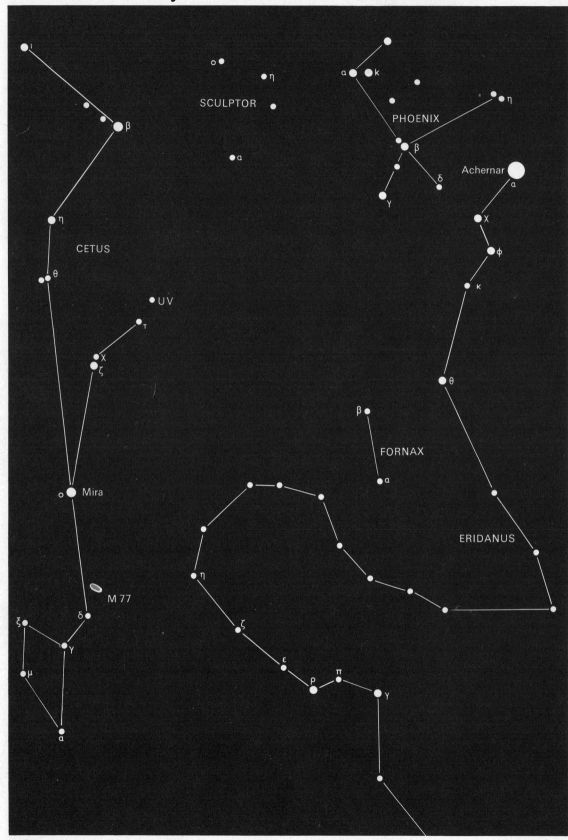

Hydrus, Carina, Columba, Lepus, Orion

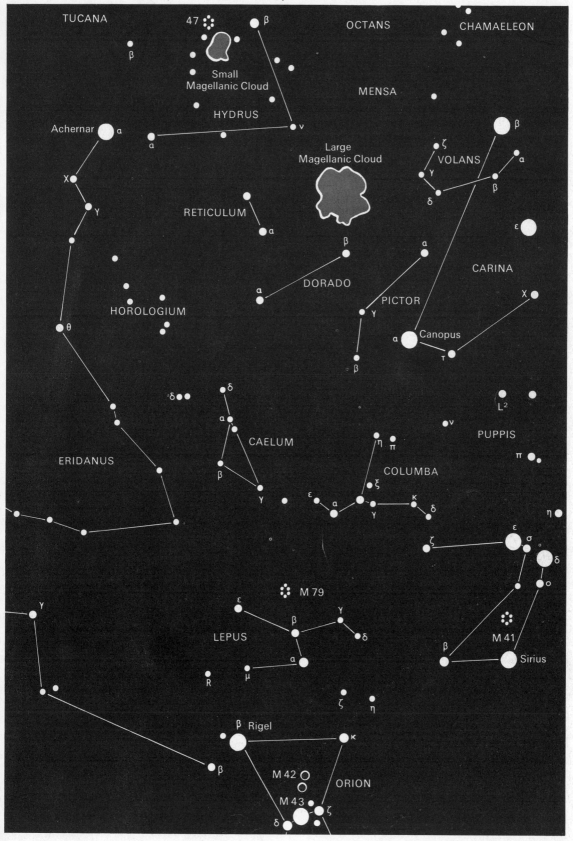

The Southern Sky 4: Notes

These maps include the two brightest stars in the sky, Sirius and Canopus, as well as Rigel in Orion and Achernar in Eridanus. The two Magellanic Clouds are in this region; we also have the globular cluster 47 Tucanæ and the most famous of all variable stars, Mira Ceti.

Sculptor. Part of this extensive but dim constellation appears on this chart. It is a blank area. The constellation includes the galactic pole.

Phoenix. The Phoenix. There is one bright star, α (Ankaa) of magnitude 2.4, but there is no really obvious pattern. β is another double with equal components; each is of the 4th magnitude, and the separation is over 1″, so that this is by no means a difficult pair.

ζ Phoenicis is a good example of an eclipsing binary. The period is 1.7 days, and since the range is from 3.6 to 4.1 the changes can be followed with the naked eye. A useful comparison star is δ, of magnitude 4.0.

Tucana. The Toucan. Though this is the faintest of the Southern Birds, it is probably the most interesting, because of three notable objects. The brightest star is α, of magnitude 2.9; next comes β, at 3.7—but any telescope will show that β is made up of two equal components, each of magnitude 4.5, at a distance of 27″. Each component is itself a close double, and there is another star in the field, of magnitude 5, which is again double.

However, Tucana is memorable chiefly for the presence of most of the Small Cloud of Magellan and for the magnificent globular cluster, 47 Tucanæ. The globular is inferior only to ω Centauri, and far exceeds the northern M.13 Herculis in splendour. It lies on the fringe of the Small Cloud; also in the immediate area is another globular, NGC 362.

To help in identifying Tucana, it is worth remembering that α Tucanæ, α Pavonis and Alnair (α Gruis) make up a triangle.

Hydrus. The Little Snake. (Translations differ; sometimes Hydra is the Sea-Serpent and Hydrus the Watersnake.) The three main stars, α, β and γ, are all of the 3rd magnitude; α lies close beside the brilliant Achernar. There are no objects in the constellation of special interest, but it is worth remembering that β Hydri is the nearest reasonably conspicuous star to the south celestial pole.

Mensa. The Table (originally Mons Mensæ, the Table Mountain). Since Mensa has no star even

as bright as the 5th magnitude, it would be perhaps the faintest constellation in the sky but for the presence of the Large Cloud of Magellan. To the casual observer, the Cloud looks rather like a detached portion of the Milky Way; it contains the great Looped Nebula, 30 Doradûs, which is visible to the naked eye.

Reticulum. The Net. Quite a compact group; α, the leading star, is below the 3rd magnitude.

Cetus. The Whale. Most of Cetus lies in the southern hemisphere, though the head is just north of the equator. Apart from α or Menkar (magnitude 2.5), which is shown on page 89, the leading star is β (Diphda), of magnitude 2.0. Diphda has been suspected of variability, though there is no proof. There would, however, be nothing surprising in this, since the spectrum is of type K and the star is decidedly orange in colour.

There is only one Messier object in Cetus: M.77. (Note, incidentally, that Eridanus, vast though it is in area, contains none at all.) M.77 lies very close to δ Ceti, though the celestial equator actually runs between them. It is a particularly interesting galaxy of the Seyfert type, with a condensed nucleus; it is a radio source, and has the distinction of being the most massive and the largest of all the spirals in Messier's list. Its distance from us is 52 million light-years, as against only 22 million light-years for the Andromeda Spiral, M.31. It is of the 9th magnitude, and so is not conspicuous in small telescopes, but it is well worth locating, and the nearness of δ Ceti makes it reasonably easy to identify.

o Ceti, or Mira, is a famous long-period variable. At its best it may reach almost the first magnitude; certainly it can outshine the Pole Star. At minimum it drops down to below magnitude 9. The period is 331 days on average, and so there are several consecutive years when maximum occurs during the season when Mira is too near the Sun to be observed. It is a red giant, and its colour is very noticeable, particularly when the star is near maximum. Though Mira is visible to the naked eye for an average of only about 18 weeks in each year, it has earned its nickname of The Wonderful.

Fornax. The Furnace. An obscure constellation adjoining Eridanus. Fornax contains a dwarf galaxy which belongs to our Local Group, but it is a very faint object.

Horologium. The Clock. Another obscure constellation, with only one star (α, 3.8) of any note.

Dorado. The Swordfish. The main point of interest is that Dorado contains part of the Large Cloud of Magellan, though most of the Cloud lies in Mensa. In Dorado the brightest star is α, magnitude 3.5. β is a Cepheid, with a range of from 3.8 to 5 and a period of 9.8 days; the fluctuations may be followed with the naked eye.

Volans. See pages 96 and 98.

Pictor. See pages 96 and 98.

Carina. See pages 96 and 98.

Eridanus. The River. The whole of this immensely long constellation is shown on the chart. It extends from Achernar, not very far from the south pole, right to β, which is close to Rigel in Orion. Achernar is the leading star; its magnitude is 0.5, and only eight stars in the entire sky outrank it. Next in order of brilliancy come β (2.8), θ (2.9) and γ (3.0).

There are not, in fact, very many telescopic objects of immediate interest. The exception is θ, or Acamar, which is a splendid double; the magnitudes of the components are 3.4 and 4.4, and the separation is over 8″.

Acamar is of interest for another reason. Astronomers of classical times, including the great Ptolemy, ranked it as of the 1st magnitude, whereas today it is only fractionally above the 3rd. Since both its components are of spectral type A, they would not be expected to show any secular change over a period of a couple of thousand years, and it seems more likely that there has been an error in interpretation or description, but the problem is certainly rather curious. Acamar was called the Last in the River; this cannot be a case of mistaken identity with Achernar—because Achernar is too far south ever to be seen from Alexandria, where Ptolemy carried out all his observations.

Much further north, and easily visible from Europe, is the star ε Eridani, of magnitude 3.7. There is nothing remarkable about its appearance; but it is one of our nearer neighbours, at only 10.8 light-years, and it is the closest star which is at all similar to the Sun. It is slightly smaller and cooler (spectral type K) and has only one third of the Sun's luminosity, but it could well be a star suitable to support a system of planets, and for this reason it and a similar star—τ Ceti, also shown on this chart—were selected as targets for a famous experiment carried out in 1960 at Green Bank, West Virginia.

The clouds of cold hydrogen in the Galaxy send out natural radio waves at a wavelength of 21.1 centimetres. Therefore, it was reasoned that any astronomers, wherever they might be, would pay attention to this particular wave-length. Suppose they decided to transmit radio signals at 21.1 centimetres, making them regular enough and rhythmical enough to show their artificial origin? The Green Bank radio team therefore 'listened out', and they concentrated upon ε Eridani and τ Ceti as being the nearest stars which might reasonably be supposed to be accompanied by a planet which could support an advanced civilization. Rather predictably, no positive results were forthcoming, and the programme was given up after a few months.

Caelum. The Sculptor's Tools (originally Caela Sculptoris). A dim, dull constellation adjoining Lepus, Eridanus and Columba. There is no star above magnitude 4½.

Columba. See pages 96 and 99.

Lepus. The Hare. A small constellation near Orion. The chief stars are α (2.6) and β (2.8); β has a companion of magnitude 9.4 at a distance of 2″.5. However, the most interesting object is R Leporis, a long-period, Mira-type variable with a period of 432 days and a magnitude range from 5.9 to 10.5. It has a spectrum of type N, and is one of the reddest stars in the sky.

Canis Major. See pages 96 and 99.

Orion. Much of this grand constellation lies in the southern hemisphere; the equator passes close to δ or Mintaka, in the Belt. Of the leaders of the constellation, only Betelgeux and Bellatrix are in the northern half of the sky. Rigel, of course, is outstandingly brilliant, and is practically the equal of Arcturus, Vega and Capella. It has a 7th-magnitude companion at a distance of 9″.2, easy to see with a 3-inch refractor and just within the range of a 2-inch. ζ, or Alnitak, the southernmost of the Belt stars, has a companion of magnitude 4.2 at a distance of 2″.4, and in the Hunter's Sword there is yet another double, ι; magnitudes 3 and 7.4, separation 11″.4.

It is in the Sword that we find M.42, the Great Nebula, the most famous object of its kind in the sky. Immersed in it is the Trapezium—the multiple star θ Orionis—whose four main components are striking even when observed with a small telescope. Recently, there have been suggestions that inside the Orion Nebula there may be stars of exceptional luminosity, almost hidden from us by the intervening nebular material.

Also in the Sword there is σ, another multiple. The magnitudes of the four principal components are 4, 7, 7.5 and 10. It is less striking than θ, but well worth examination.

INDEX